SECOND EDITION

# Learning Power

## STRATEGIES FOR STUDENT SUCCESS

*Dave Ellis and Peter Lenn*

# nmsa

*National Middle School Association is dedicated to improving the educational experiences of young adolescents by providing vision, knowledge, and resources to all who serve them in order to develop healthy, productive, and ethical citizens.*

*In pursuit of this mission, NMSA has joined with Learning Technologies to provide materials and services to ensure student success.* Learning Power: Strategies for Student Success *and* The Learning Power Workbook *are endorsed by NMSA which is committed to empowering students to become independent, life-long learners. The strategies presented in this book can assist in achieving that goal.*

*Learning Power: Strategies for Student Success* by Dave Ellis & Peter Lenn
Second Edition

*Editors:* Larry M. David & Mary Maisey-Ireland
*Contributing Editor:* Doug Toft
*Cover & Graphic Design:* Jeff Swaim
*Production & Layout:* Kim Oslund
*Illustration:* S. Robert Beers
*Photography:* Mike Wolforth & Jim Osborne
*Cover Photo:* Phil Ertel

Learning Technologies
*Permissions*
2650 Jackson Boulevard
Rapid City, SD 57702.
Phone: 800-457-2913

Printed in the U.S.A.
ISBN: 0-9638133-3-1
1 2 3 4 5 6 7 8 BA 98 97 96 95

# Table of Contents

# Chapter 1 Objectives

After mastering this chapter you will be able to:

- DEFINE SUCCESS FOR YOURSELF

- APPLY THE MASTERY LEARNING PROCESS TO YOUR STUDIES

- USE THE CHANGE PROCESS TO DEVELOP EFFECTIVE HABITS

# CHAPTER 1 GETTING STARTED

# Meet Learning Power...

**L**EARNING POWER and *The Learning Power Workbook* are about thinking, writing, and changing the way you do things. You can use these tools to be more effective at studying, taking tests, doing math, writing, improving your memory, managing your time, speaking in public, getting along with other people, and much more.

Adopt a few of the methods in this book, and you will see immediate results. Get more done in less time and with less effort. Approach tests with more confidence. Set goals to help you reach your dreams through actions you can take today. These are just a few of the benefits waiting for you when you think, write, and practice.

Use this book to make the time you spend on schoolwork pay off. Once you experience success with some of these methods, you'll probably decide to experiment with more. You might even discover that you like school better. At each step of the way, it will be up to you to choose how much of this book to use. The more you use *Learning Power*, the more you will gain.

# and The Learning Power Workbook

T*HE LEARNING POWER Workbook* invites you to become a co-author of this textbook. That's because *Learning Power* isn't finished. What you see already written is important. But equally important is what you write. That's the value of the workbook.

This course is about taking action. Do whatever it takes to make *The Learning Power Workbook* a record of your thinking and your progress. Underline. Highlight. Mark. Deface. Scribble in the margins. Disagree. Doodle. Fill it up.

Workbook symbols, like the ones that follow, appear throughout *Learning Power*. When these symbols appear, it is your cue to do the indicated activity in the workbook.

## JOURNAL

When making Journal Entries, take a few moments to examine what you think or feel about the topic and write down your thoughts. Your writing will not be graded, so don't worry about grammar or spelling for these exercises. There are no right or wrong answers in Journal Entries.

## PRACTICE

This is perhaps the most valuable activity of all. Practice leads to excellence. The practice exercises give you hands-on experience with the techniques suggested in *Learning Power*. The cycle of practicing something and then discovering how you did can help you improve in any area you desire.

Throughout *Learning Power* you'll find references to workbook Practices.

Doing the Practices can make the difference between a suggestion or idea that stays with you and one that dies right on the page. Use Practices to stay active, awake, and involved.

## KEY WORDS

These highlighted words and concepts will expand your vocabulary by focusing on particular words and phrases that have special meaning.

## OUTLINE

A great way to learn any material is to re-create it in outline form. You will outline each chapter, and sometimes individual articles, and learn to use several outlining methods.

## PROGRESS CHECK

Mastering each assignment before going on to the next is more important than studying a large number of chapters or techniques in a given amount of time. Don't worry about being faster or slower than anyone else. If you put in the time you need to master each assignment, your learning rate will increase and you will build your learning power.

When you complete each chapter, consider whether you have mastered all of the material and skills. When both you and your teacher are convinced that you have mastered the chapter, you are ready to go on to the next step.

# Exercise

*Please experiment with a new behavior that can become a habit. Look at every page in this book and the workbook. Get a sense of what the whole thing is about before you zero in on any of the parts.*

*Reading experts agree that one of the most effective strategies for getting more out of a book is to look it over before you read it. Please take this action now.*

WORKBOOK
JOURNAL 1-1

# Make This Book Your Coach

IN MANY WAYS *Learning Power* looks like an ordinary book. It has titles, subtitles, and paragraphs. It offers ideas and asks you to think. Yet this book is different from most books you'll ever read. *Learning Power* asks for your energy. Use it well, and you'll burn some calories. That happens as you take action, think, write, and practice what you have learned.

A book is a poor substitute for a good friend or a skilled teacher. You will learn things in a well-taught course that aren't in *Learning Power*. On the other hand, this book is available to you twenty-four hours a day, every day. It will never scold, argue, or criticize. It's always ready with words of encouragement. Make friends with this book, and it can become your faithful coach for success.

You will get the most out of *Learning Power* by using the following suggestions.

## USE IT EVERY DAY

Even if you spend only five minutes, take some time each day to apply at least one idea or hint. Regular practice improves our skills at whatever we do—playing the guitar, playing basketball, dancing, you name it. The same thing is true for using these ideas. Five minutes may not sound like a lot of time, but it adds up to over thirty hours of practice in a year. That's enough time to learn some new habits that will help make you successful.

## JUMP AROUND

With your teacher's assistance, choose the chapters that will help you the most. If you want advice about a particular technique, you can skip to that section and learn about it at any time.

## PUT IT INTO PRACTICE

The ideas in this book have been tested by your peers—other people who need to take notes, read books, score well on tests, manage their time, and do all the other things that make one successful in school.

Test these strategies in your other classes. You don't have to believe any of the ideas; just use them. Experiment and see what works. For example, when the book suggests talking out loud to memorize, give it a shot.

## INVOLVE OTHERS

You might think that studying is something you do alone while trapped behind a big door marked *"Do Not Disturb."* Just the opposite is often most effective. You can enlist other students in your efforts to succeed in school. Form study groups that meet both in and out of class.

Explain a subject to one of your classmates, and you'll understand it in a new way. One of the best ways to learn something is to teach it. Working with others moves you into action. That makes a big difference in what you remember and what you use.

## DEMAND A LOT

Scour this book for ideas about mastering your courses, overcoming procrastination, catching up in subjects in which you are behind, and working out problems with your parents and teachers.

When you don't understand something, ask questions. Use the techniques so you discover what really works for you. The time you spend doing this can change this book from a couple hundred pages of paper into a blueprint for your academic success.

WORKBOOK
JOURNAL 1-2

# Define Success

**S**UCCESS IS A MATTER of interpretation. One person's definition includes money or fame. Another's might involve plenty of time for having fun. Someone else's idea of success is feeding the world's hungry or saving the rain forests. Chances are that your family, teachers, and friends, have their ideas about what you should do to be successful. This book is designed to help you reach your own goals, whatever they may be. Your own measure of success will carry the most weight.

Beware of defining your success by the success of others. Comparison can ruin your feelings of success and lead to dissatisfaction. There will always be someone who has more or performs better. Don't worry about how others choose to measure their success or how they measure yours. Go for what you want.

WORKBOOK
JOURNAL 1-3

# Improve Your Skills

**S**UCCEEDING IN SCHOOL usually means mastering three types of skills. First, there are the basic skills, often called the "three R's"— reading, 'riting, and 'rithmetic. Second, there are study skills, things like taking notes, handling tests, and memorizing. The third area includes self-management skills—things like setting goals, managing time, staying motivated, and communicating with others.

These three categories of skills make a difference in school and in the rest of your life too.

*Learning Power* coaches you to increase your ability in all three areas. It also suggests ways to practice these skills so you can master them. When you master something, you don't worry about memorizing the guidelines. Mastery becomes your habitual way to learn.

WORKBOOK PRACTICE 1-4

## Basic Skills

Reading: speed, comprehension, and vocabulary

Math: calculations, fractions, decimals, percentages, word problems

Writing: grammar, vocabulary, spelling, penmanship, typing, word processing

## Study Skills

Getting information and ideas from a textbook

Memorizing written passages

Memorizing facts

Taking notes

Taking tests

Using the library

Writing essays and term papers

Problem solving

Learning math

## Self-Management Skills

Gaining awareness: spotting what's working and what's not in your life

Setting goals: writing down your long-term and short-term goals

Managing your time

Mastering homework assignments

Noting your successes

Changing your own behavior or habits

Speaking in public

Learning with a tutor

Communicating with peers, teachers, and parents

Making and keeping agreements

# Check Your Mindset

M IND•SET (mind'set') n. 1. A fixed mental attitude or disposition that predetermines a person's responses to and interpretations of situations. 2. An inclination or habit.

The following six statements make up a mindset that will serve you well in achieving your goals.

1. I DESERVE TO BE SUCCESSFUL.
Every day is a new opportunity. Success is not in short supply. For you to succeed, someone else doesn't have to fail.

2. I AM INTELLIGENT ENOUGH TO MASTER MY COURSES.
Intelligence is really a combination of natural ability plus the effects of previous learning and practice. People who have practiced a lot in a subject appear to be more intelligent. Your intelligence is very likely more than adequate.

3. I AM AN INDIVIDUAL WITH MY OWN LEARNING RATES.
The rate at which you learn one subject may differ from the rate at which you learn another. Your rate might be faster or slower than that of others who are learning the same subject. This is not a sign that you or they lack intelligence. It means only that you have your own learning rate in each area.

## 4. I AM RESPONSIBLE FOR MY OWN EDUCATION.

Other people, such as your parents, guardians, and teachers have responsibility too. You have the most at stake, and you control the most important factors. If you are dissatisfied with your education, you can change what you are doing. You can also wish for others to change. You may even be able to persuade them to change. But you have far more control over what *you* do. What you do is the most important factor in your learning.

## 5. I CAN ACHIEVE SUCCESS BY:
Planning
Preparing
Practicing to mastery
Getting prompt feedback

In this book you will find out how to use these steps in different courses.

## 6. I CAN MAKE TOMORROW'S ASSIGNMENT EASIER.

Some students seem to get "A's" effortlessly. Look more closely, and you'll find people who invested time in mastering the **prerequisites** and early lessons in the subject. Learning is **cumulative**. Their time investment may be more or less than yours. That's not important. What matters is doing what helps you succeed today.

WORKBOOK
PRACTICE 1-5

# Discover Mastery Learning

ERHAPS THE MOST powerful approach to learning is mastering one step before going on to the next. Mastering a skill means that you are competent, that you can definitely perform or demonstrate that skill. Once you have mastered addition, you are ready, willing, and able to pass any reasonable test in adding. You could even show others how to add. That's the idea of mastery. It means you are capable and confident.

Mastery learning has a number of advantages. Learning gets faster and easier as you go along. With **mastery learning** you not only learn more easily and quickly, you also retain the material longer. Mastering the material gives you a sense of progress and success. You may start to enjoy learning subjects that previously were a drag.

For example, in arithmetic you learn addition, then subtraction, multiplication, and so on. Mastering addition reduces the time and effort needed to learn subtraction. If you try to learn subtraction before you've mastered addition, learning subtraction can take longer or even be impossible. That is why, once you fall behind in a course, it is so difficult to catch up.

The graph below indicates that mastering one step decreases the time needed for learning the next step. In other words, it may take some time to master the first few assignments. As your learning rate increases, your learning per hour begins to zoom upward.

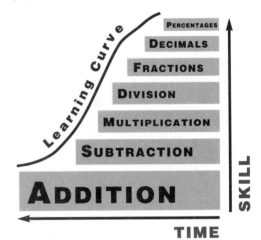

Each of us has our own learning rate in each area of life. Our learning curves have the same general shape, but they are not identical. Learning curves vary for many reasons, including difference in age, experience, and attitudes. At any given time, your learning rate may be faster or slower than others'.

Mastering an assignment may at times take longer than expected. That may mean it takes you longer than someone else, or longer than the teacher's estimate, or longer than you would like. Still, the extra time spent now to master any assignment will save time on later assignments. Mastery learning almost always takes less time overall and leads to more learning and higher grades.

In most classes teachers don't stay on each topic until everyone has mastered it. Still, you can use mastery learning to be sure that you have mastered each assignment. That might mean putting in more than the usual amount of time for a while. If you'll make that extra effort, you can expect to see the benefits quickly.

## INTELLIGENCE

You may wonder if you are smart enough to master all of your schoolwork. What if you practiced forever and still couldn't reach the goal? That makes it important to know, up front, whether you can master your assignments.

Consider this. Almost everyone learns to speak and understand their native language, yet they often balk at learning a second language. A "foreign" language is really just one we never learned as infants. We are probably as capable of learning a language as the infants who live where that language is spoken. To be incapable of learning a

particular language, we would have to be less intelligent than everyone who has ever learned it. That's not likely.

Several studies indicate that most students—over 90 percent—have enough intelligence to master all of the high school curriculum. This is more than just passing courses; it means really mastering the subjects. To put it plainly, it is almost certain that you are smart enough to succeed in school.

## MOTIVATION

Some students think they have intelligence but lack a mysterious quality called **motivation**. They believe there is something about them that makes it difficult to like school and learning. They might be described as "unmotivated."

Motivation is simply a desire to attain something coupled with a belief that it is possible to attain it. Most people like doing things that they do well. They're motivated to do tasks, even difficult tasks, so long as they believe that succeeding is both possible and worthwhile.

As mastery learning begins to bring the results you want, your motivation jumps. You may never like studying better than you like talking to your friends on the phone. By applying this method, your motivation for studying can grow.

# Set the Stage

**I**F LACK OF INTELLIGENCE and motivation aren't the problems, what can you do to have more success in school? Here are three suggestions:

## LEARN TO STUDY EFFECTIVELY

**1** Just because they spend years in school, students don't automatically know the best ways to study. Students learn or invent their own methods. Some of those methods work well; others do not. This book includes techniques used by successful students. Many of them can work for you too. You might even find a few that make a big difference in your experience of school.

## PRACTICE SUCCEEDING

**2** No matter what has happened in the past, you can succeed. Maybe you've gotten behind, or received low grades, or had teachers you didn't like. When these things happen, students may think something is wrong with them. They feel discouraged, and that gets in the way of learning. School seems more and more difficult. If any of this is true for you, this course may help you see that you can succeed. You can watch yourself master assignments and build confidence in your ability to succeed.

## OVERCOME YOUR RESISTANCE

**3** Most of us resent being told what to do. This is especially true when trying to establish independence—particularly with parents and teachers. Resistance gets confused with independence. In this course you can learn some ways to move through resistance without giving up your independence. You may even gain more freedom by being more successful in school.

# Take Four Steps to Mastery

THE HABIT OF GOING for mastery is one of the most useful habits in learning. To get a handle on this method, plan, prepare, practice, and get feedback.

## 1. PLAN FOR MASTERY

Knowing where you want to go greatly increases the odds of getting there. If you don't know what the goal is, you might stop too soon or end up spending your time on the wrong track. Planning involves setting a goal and scheduling actions that will move you toward it.

## 2. PREPARE TO PRACTICE

Before you practice, it helps to know what is required of you, along with what and how to practice. You can get this by listening, reading, or watching a demonstration. Much of the listening and watching you do in class is preparation for practice you do later at home or during study hall. Reading a textbook or your notes is preparation. The practice comes next.

## 3. PRACTICE TO MASTERY

Most skills call for more than just reading or gathering information. Meeting our goals usually means taking some action as well. For the pianist it's practicing scales. For the tennis pro it's practicing a backhand stroke. For students it includes many types of practice activities, such as solving problems, doing experiments, writing essays, or speaking another language.

## 4. GET PROMPT FEEDBACK

Feedback lets you know how well your practice is going. In some situations you can see this for yourself. At other times, crucial feedback comes from teachers, tutors, quizzes, or study partners.

WORKBOOK PRACTICE 1-6

Y OU CAN BECOME skillful at almost anything by practicing, from tuning a car engine to tuning a guitar. It's also true of the things you do in school. Becoming skillful at solving math problems or writing essays is a matter of practice. So are learning spelling, vocabulary, grammar, history, and science.

# Practice, Practice, Practice

You probably spend most of your time in class listening to others. That includes listening to your teachers and to other students. Even if you participate actively and pay attention, you don't get much time to practice during the school day. Thirty minutes of homework for a course will generally provide much more practice time than a fifty minute class period. This is why homework is so important.

Many of the techniques in this book are intended to help you to do your homework—that is, to practice.

These techniques include powerful ways to practice for different subjects, overcome procrastination, concentrate and be efficient, know when you have practiced enough to master and retain material, and much more. Using the strategies in this book can give you "learning power."

# Overcome Stage Fright

**M**OST PEOPLE are afraid to speak in public. Getting comfortable speaking to an audience is an amazing experience. When you succeed at this (yes, you can), the benefits will extend to many other parts of your life. That's why your teacher may include getting beyond the fear of public speaking as part of this course.

The overcoming stage fright process of a *Learning Power* student success course has three purposes:

1. To build your self-confidence. Succeeding at something that previously scared us changes the way we think about ourselves. Embarrassment and discomfort need not stop us from practicing a skill to mastery.

2. To demonstrate that mastery learning works on challenging tasks by mastering one small step after another.

3. To assist you to overcome fear of public speaking, to enable you to say what you think, calmly. Examples are speaking in class, to a teacher, to adults, to large groups, or to parents.

Mastery learning makes overcoming stage fright possible by breaking up the public speaking process into many small parts. These are practiced one step at a time, and your comfort and confidence are achieved at each level before moving on.

You can use this same process to overcome fear of almost any activity— climbing to high places, taking tests, handling animals, performing music, or driving a car.

T HERE'S AN IDEA that's been held through the ages by spiritual leaders, counselors, business leaders—and successful students. The idea is simple: Success begins with knowing yourself.

# Know Yourself

When looking at ourselves, we have a choice of methods. One is to focus on what should be: "I should be better at reading. I should have studied more last semester. I should be better at taking tests. I should have different friends. I should weigh less." The list is endless. Soon it seems as if we can never measure up.

Another option is to forget "what I should be" and discover "who I am today." This means telling the truth about what's happening right now—without shame or blame. Telling the truth frees up energy and sets the stage for changes to occur.

The Personal Profile in *The Learning Power Workbook* is a way to size up how you are doing in five areas: goals and plans, study skills, homework, motivation and attitude, and health and well-being. It is not a test. It is a way to ask yourself important questions and to tell the truth about the kind of student you are today. Use the Personal Profile to help you notice the things you do well, along with the things you want to improve.

When completing the Personal Profile exercise, keep two suggestions in mind. First, think of this exercise as a starting point—the first rung on the ladder of success. Second, don't be too serious. It's OK to laugh at yourself; a sense of humor may help you be more truthful. Don't worry about looking good. When you reach the end of the book, you can repeat this exercise and see how you've changed.

WORKBOOK
JOURNAL 1-7

# Adopt a Process for Change

MOST OF US can list areas in our lives where things aren't working as well as we would like. Often there are many things we would like to change. Some people say, "I can't change. That's just the way I am." Others may say, "I'm not the problem. There's someone else who is messing me up. I want that person to change."

Here are alternative ways of looking at those two situations. Instead of saying, "It's my nature," we might say, "It's just a habit, so I can change it." Changing a long-term habit may not be easy, but at least it sounds possible.

Getting someone else to change can be tough. You may have tried polite requests, persuasion, or even threats, and had little success. To get someone else to change, try changing yourself. It may seem unfair that you, not the other person, have to change. It may seem like giving in or selling out. If what you have done in the past hasn't worked, change what you can control—namely, yourself.

When you try to change a habit, it may be embarrassing or feel peculiar for a while. Here's a method you might add to your tool kit for success — the Change Process.

Like any method, the Change Process doesn't fit every situation. Many people have found it helpful, and you may too. Even if you don't follow the specific steps listed below, you can act on their general ideas.

## STEP 1: AWARENESS

Begin by simply noticing what is going on—usually a behavior you don't like. Then tell the truth about that behavior without judging it or putting yourself down. If this seems hard—well, telling the truth takes real courage. When you make it this far, congratulate yourself.

## STEP 2: RESPONSIBILITY

Now take responsibility for the current situation. Asking yourself a couple of questions may help: "How could I be helping to create this event? What am I doing before, during, and after this happens?" Sometimes the problem is not what we do but what we fail to do.

It can be hard to stay objective during this process. Imagine how someone else would describe your role in the problem. The only purpose here is to discover what isn't working. Once you have a clear picture of that, go to Step 3.

## Step 3: Forgiveness

Forgive yourself for the way things have been up to now. Be as gentle with yourself as you would be with a loved one who did the same thing. Even when you make mistakes, you are OK. The Perfect Human Being Society is a club with no members.

## Step 4: Change

Start doing something differently. It doesn't have to be something big. Often the simplest, smallest changes have the biggest results. Brainstorm some options. To get ideas, talk to a person who has succeeded in a situation like yours.

## Step 5: Practice

Practice the new behavior until you master it. Sometimes this is tough because the new way of acting feels uncomfortable. What's more, it may not be effective for a while. Don't be surprised if you slip into your old behavior. When you notice this, forgive yourself and then continue practicing the new behavior.

## Step 6: Feedback

Determine if what you are doing is working and getting you closer to your goal. If not, go to Step 2 and cycle through the process again. Be gentle with yourself, and be honest. Most of the time you've got nothing to lose but an old habit.

HABITS TO START
Remembering to tell Mom
    where I am
Saving money
Creating a stronger body
Remembering to make my bed
    and hang up my clothes

HABITS TO STOP
Biting my nails
Saying "um" and "you know"
Twisting the phone cord
Leaving cans and dishes
    on the coffee table

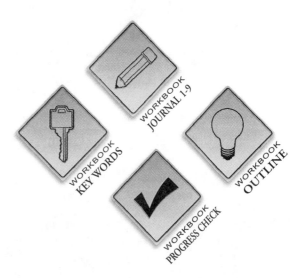

# Take Note of Your Success

**A** SUCCESS LOG is a written record of what you have accomplished—a kind of personal report card. It is important that you write down only your successes, not your failures. As you work toward your goals, you get feedback from others. That's external feedback. In addition, you evaluate yourself—internal feedback.

You will benefit from giving yourself credit for your successes. If you write them down, you make them that much more powerful. A Success Log can be just a piece of paper or a special book or diary. Notice how you are doing. When you have succeeded, give yourself positive, accurate feedback.

Many people write and speak about the importance of self-esteem. Self-esteem can be hard to define. One way to think about this issue is to borrow an idea from psychologist Nathaniel Branden. He defines self-esteem as "the reputation we acquire about ourselves." In other words, self-esteem refers to how we think of ourselves. Given this definition, our self-esteem could be high or low. Feedback we get—both external and internal—plays a big role here.

A Success Log can change the way you think about yourself. It also keeps your goals in view and boosts your energy level. Success Logs don't call for lying about yourself or overstating your accomplishments. It's simply a matter of taking credit for your progress.

# Chapter 2 Objectives

After mastering this chapter
you will be able to:

- IDENTIFY AND SET
  PERSONAL GOALS

- MANAGE YOUR TIME
  EFFECTIVELY

- FOCUS YOUR
  ATTENTION

# CHAPTER TIME 2

# Set Your Goals

ONE REASON people don't get what they want is that they don't know what they want. The first step in planning is to choose your dreams—where you want to go or what you wish to accomplish. You can then find ways to connect what you are doing in school right now with your future. Knowing where you are going can increase your enthusiasm and boost your energy level.

It may seem hard to know where to begin. It helps to step back and think in terms of the "big picture"and then move toward the details. With that in mind, let's look at three kinds of goals.

## SET LONG-TERM GOALS FIRST

Most of us have some notions of what we want in life—things like being happy, having a career, making money, having a family, or seeing the world. These visions can be the starting point for defining your **long-term** and **life goals**. These goals will probably take more than one year to achieve. They may take five, or even twenty-five, years.

One way to start is to brainstorm. Imagine your life in ten or twenty years. Where will you be? Who will be with you? How you will spend your day? As you let your mind roam, notice your thoughts and images. Jot them down. Leave evaluation for later. Following are examples of long-term goals.

Graduate from high school
Travel around the world
Get married
Manage a restaurant
Own a body shop
Play baseball with the Blue Jays
Make a million dollars
Play drums in a rock band
Own a Harley-Davidson
Teach in a college
Direct movies
Find a cure for cancer
Work in environmental
    engineering
Become a doctor
Fly airplanes
Be a cartoonist

Your goals aren't right or wrong, and you don't have to have them all figured out. You may not have decided on your career or about having a family. That's OK. Also, expect your long-term plans to change as you learn more about yourself and the world.

## SET INTERMEDIATE GOALS

Intermediate goals are those you can accomplish in one year or less—goals that will move you toward your long-term goals. Here are some examples of intermediate goals:

> Learn three new dances this term
> Buy a used computer
> Earn a 3.5 grade point average this term
> Get an "A" in Spanish
> Work up a good curve ball
> Take a metalworking class
> Audition for the school play
> Apply to Space Camp
> Save money for a helicopter ride

## SET DAILY AND WEEKLY GOALS

Achieving anything in life takes direction and action. Daily and weekly goals tell you exactly what you can do today to move toward your dreams. While you might achieve a long-term or intermediate goal during some weeks, most daily and weekly goals are small steps toward those longer-range goals. Here are some examples of daily or weekly goals:

> Do all my chores
> Complete assigned Spanish homework for this week
> Work several hours and save $20 toward a helicopter ride
> Research a Community Ed computer course
> Try two new recipes for family dinners
> Clean my room by the weekend
> Practice pitching baseballs for one-half hour a day

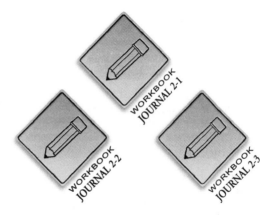

WORKBOOK JOURNAL 2-1
WORKBOOK JOURNAL 2-2
WORKBOOK JOURNAL 2-3

# Track Your Time

**M**ANAGING TIME may sound like all work and no play, but effective time managers can be relaxed, joyous, and efficient all at the same time. Skill at scheduling enables you to reach your goals without feeling rushed or bored.

People often ask, "Where did all the hours (or days, weeks, months, years) go?" One of the most powerful ways to manage your time is to answer that very question. Before scheduling or making major changes in the way you spend your time, track it for a while to get to know your habits.

The way you use time is unique and personal. A time-management strategy that works wonders for someone else may be completely off track for you. Tracking your time will help guide your choices about its management and make an immediate difference in your life.

Carry a few 3x5 cards in your pocket. Whenever you start a new activity, write down a word or two describing that activity and the time you started it. You can use a calendar for the same purpose.

If you have access to a computer, consider using a time planning program. The form in Chapter 2 of *The Learning Power Workbook* is another device you can use for tracking your time.

Tracking your time needs to take only a few minutes each day. Before you go to bed, note what you did during each hour of that day. If you're not 100 percent accurate, don't worry about it. Just get as close as you can.

> Tuesday 10/12
> 6:15 Get ready for school
> 6:45 Breakfast
> 7:00 Chores
> 7:20 Bus
> 7:50 School - friends
> 8:05 Classes
> 11:25 Lunch

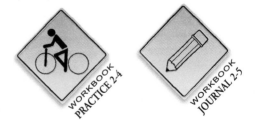

WORKBOOK PRACTICE 2-4

WORKBOOK JOURNAL 2-5

# Plan Your Time

ONCE YOU KNOW more about how you spend time, consider taking charge of your time in ways that get you more of what you want. Use these general suggestions to discover what works for you:

## 1. SET REALISTIC GOALS AND SCHEDULES

Expecting to complete a four-hour job in two hours can be a set up for failure. So can trying to fit 169 hours of activity into one week. School is a full-time job. When including both class time and homework in your schedule, you're likely to find that school takes about forty hours a week.

When you add in time to sleep, eat, and relax, you may discover it's not possible to do all the things you'd like to do. Balancing your schedule often means choosing among recreation, hobbies, school events, sports, or a job.

Many students are as busy, if not busier, than their parents. Being realistic about your time commitments is an act of kindness to yourself.

## 2. ADJUST YOUR SCHEDULE TO MATCH YOUR GOALS

You may have discovered that you're spending too much time doing things you don't enjoy or that don't help you to reach your goals, or both. Build activities into your plan that contribute to your goals and happiness.

## 3. GET ENOUGH SLEEP

Sleep deprivation is common among young people. To be healthy and maintain a clear mind, you may need nine or ten hours of sleep every night. Cutting down on sleep is the wrong way to find more time.

When you are tired, tasks—especially trying to learn—might take you longer. You might pass the quiz tomorrow but forget what you learned within a week. If lack of sleep makes you sick, you can lose more time than you save.

## 4. SCHEDULE TEN HOURS OF HOMEWORK A WEEK

Depending on which grade you are in, you can expect up to two hours of homework a night. Some elective courses may have no homework, while drama or sports may require a lot of time.

During some weeks you might complete all of your current assignments in less than two hours per night. Major projects, term papers, and book reports take much longer than other assignments. To avoid overload in the wee hours just before they are due, allow time for them each week.

## 5. Avoid Marathon Study Sessions

Doing your Spanish an hour a day for a week is usually easier and more effective than doing six hours of Spanish on Sunday. When you schedule yourself for a six hour marathon, it is hard to stay focused and efficient.

When possible, study in short sessions. If you have much work to do, break your time into short blocks of twenty to forty minutes. Take five- or ten-minute breaks, and alternate your blocks of study time among different subjects.

## 6. Schedule Time for Fun

Fun is important—an investment in your health and happiness. It pays to "waste" time once in a while.

## 7. Leave Open Space in Your Schedule

Unexpected things happen. Use uncommitted time to handle emergencies, catch up, or seize new opportunities.

## 8. Plan to Plan

Schedule ten minutes each evening to write in your Success Log and to plan your time for tomorrow.

Once a week, perhaps on Sunday evenings, do your weekly planning. Another option is to plan on Friday afternoons, preventing the unpleasant possibility of a forgotten assignment due on Monday.

## 9. Allow Time for Chores and Errands

Don't forget tasks such as doing dishes, walking your dog, taking out the garbage, and other routine jobs.

WORKBOOK PRACTICE 2-6

WORKBOOK PRACTICE 2-7

# Keep To-Do Lists

**K**EEPING TRACK of things to do is essential for success in school or anywhere else. If you want to stay organized, write down assignments on Assignment Sheets in your school binder. Note specifically what is due and when it is due. To further refine your plan, write down which assignments and other things you plan to do today on a daily **To-Do List**.

There are several options for keeping this list. Three-by-five index cards are handy. You can write To-Do Items in your calendar. In any case, keep this list with you and add new items as they come up. Cross off items as you complete them. This is the fun part of keeping a To-Do List.

Write out your new list each night for the following day. The next morning you will be ready to go.

Some tasks are urgent, and others can be delayed. Some require a fixed amount of time, while others last indefinitely. If you find your list getting long or scary, here's a suggestion.

Rate each task on the list with a **priority** of "A," "B," or "C." The "A" items are most important—things that are due now or that need immediate action. The "B" tasks are less important or less urgent at the moment. A book report due in a week may have a "B" priority today but have an "A" priority next week. However, reading the book is probably an "A" task this week. "C" items don't require immediate attention.

"C" tasks (organizing your dresser drawers or alphabetizing your compact disk collection) are often easier or more interesting than "B's" and "A's." Beware: "C" tasks can steal you away from your more important activities. After ranking the priority of your To-Do Items, you might decide to delete some "C's" altogether.

WORKBOOK PRACTICE 2-8

# Exercise

*Create your To-Do List now. On an index card or in your calendar, write all the things you need to do between now and tomorrow night. If you think of things you need to do in the future, write them on a separate card or page.*

*Once you have your list, rate the priority of each item as "A," "B," or "C." Finally, look over the list of goals you made earlier in this chapter and see if there are any other things you could be doing today, or in the near future, to reach those goals. If so, add them to your To-Do list. Enjoy the feeling of creating your future and taking charge of your life—now.*

## Ask Some Timely Questions

Answering the following questions is one way to focus your attention and manage time like a professional.

1. At this moment, am I doing what I want to do  or what I agreed to do?

2. Am I doing this to avoid doing something else?

3. Is there something I could do right now to move me toward my goals?

4. Am I doing this task well enough or too well?

5. Do I need a little more time and effort to do it right?

6. Do I have a good reason for doing this?

7. Am I taking responsibility for what is happening?

8. Am I blaming others for things I could change myself?

9. Who could help me with this?

10. Am I neglecting other things that I want to do?

11. If I really wanted to, could I do this?

12. If someone paid me $1,000 to get this done, could I find time for it?

# Overcome Procrastination

**P**ROCRASTINATION and school assignments tend to go hand in hand. Procrastination means to put off doing something. It is an expensive habit and it can eat away at your enjoyment of the present moment. You may spend more time worrying about not doing something than you would spending just doing it.

Here are some suggestions. Make a clear decision either to do a task or not to do it. If you are having trouble deciding, look at the task in relation to your goals. If you decide to do it, follow through. There's real pleasure in knowing that you can rely on yourself. If you decide not to do the task, congratulate yourself for saving time.

Put any things you have been avoiding on your To-Do List. Set specific times for doing them. To sweeten the deal, choose a reward for getting the task done—perhaps playing a video game, watching TV, or calling a friend.

Take the reward only when you've earned it. Create your own cheering section by surrounding yourself with people who applaud, stamp their feet, and whistle when you get things done and meet your goals.

WORKBOOK PRACTICE 2-9

# Be Aware

ONE MOMENT you're listening to a teacher in class, and the next moment you're thinking about your plans for Saturday night. One moment you're reading a magazine, and the next second your attention is on the music coming from another room. Your **point of attention**, or awareness, is moving around.

Your awareness will often shift without any apparent reason. The shifts described above are more or less accidental. Because your brain can out-perform a supercomputer, you have another option. You can intentionally remove your attention from one thing and choose to focus on something else.

When you bring your attention to the task at hand, you are obviously more effective. Yet it's hard to focus on some tasks. Concentrating on a good movie is easy. It might be more diffi-cult to stay focused on schoolwork.

Try paying attention to yourself. For example, when your attention drifts from your book to a phone call, notice that this is happening. Being self-aware is different from being self-conscious. **Self-awareness** can make you more comfortable with yourself and assist you to develop new capabilities.

As you notice your attention shifting away from what you are doing, bring your attention back to the task and continue. You may also decide to drop the original task and focus on the new one. Make the choice consciously.

Unconscious shifts in awareness may sometimes happen for a reason. By noticing when your awareness moves away from what you are doing, you may discover a pattern at work within yourself. One student was frequently distracted while working on her math assignments. She noticed that everything was fine until she got into a problem that she couldn't easily handle. Then her attention would shift.

This student came to realize that she felt stupid and afraid every time she came across a difficult math problem. Whenever those feelings surfaced, she immediately tried to escape by shifting her attention to snacks, the phone, a magazine, or the TV. By understanding what triggered her wandering attention, she dramatically improved her ability to keep her mind on her math problems.

# Exercise

*To practice directing your awareness to whatever you choose, try this. Think of the last time you ate an apple. Next, think of a teacher you liked. Now remember a time when you were having fun. Now move your awareness to the people or things in the room with you. Finally, notice that you were able to direct your awareness.*

*Before continuing, take a moment to focus your attention on something you are going to do later today. Then bring your awareness back to this book and continue reading.*

# Chapter 3 Objectives

After mastering this chapter you will be able to:

- IDENTIFY THREE PATHWAYS TO MASTERY

- ORGANIZE YOUR HOMEWORK SPACE AND MATERIALS

- APPLY A FOUR-STEP PROCESS FOR COMPLETING ASSIGNMENTS

# CHAPTER 3 PREPARE FOR PRACTICE

# Think of Homework as Practice

THE ASPIRING concert pianist could spend hours listening to lectures about how to play the piano. But, if she really wants to master the instrument, she'll be at the keyboard every day. The aspiring baseball star could sit around all day talking about how to throw curve balls. That would be a poor substitute for time on the pitcher's mound. In each case, mastery calls not only for understanding but also for action. That's another name for practice.

School works the same way. While in class, you may not get much time to practice. For most of the day, you probably listen to teachers and to other students asking questions or reciting. During six hours in school, you may get only ten or fifteen minutes of actual practice. In comparison, two hours of homework gives you about ten times as much practice. Homework is a big part of your success.

If we learn by practicing but don't practice much in school, why spend time in class? Class time prepares us for practice. The teacher demonstrates and explains what you are to learn and goes over assignments. And you get feedback to find out if your practice is on track or if you need additional help.

WORKBOOK
JOURNAL 3-1

# Memorize, Perform, and Solve

**T**HIS CHAPTER returns to the key idea that success in learning requires practice to mastery. The most appropriate kind of practice will depend on the subject and your teacher. Here are three types of practice:

Memorizing
Performing
Solving problems

## MEMORIZING

Many courses involve **memorizing** facts, dates, names, words, formulas, or ideas. This is all information that provides a base for later learning. You memorize when you need to know facts right off the top of your head. Examples include:

Number of days in each
month and in a year
Multiplication tables
Names of parts of the body
Vocabulary and spelling
Names and locations of
states, countries, continents.
Historic dates, people,
and events

## PERFORMING

Although you may first need to memorize information, such as facts about the activity, **performing** calls for doing—taking some action.
Here are some examples of performing:

Writing a story
Taking tests
Speaking a foreign language
Speaking in public
Typing
Adding and subtracting

## SOLVING PROBLEMS

Finally, you can practice by solving problems. The difference between performing and problem solving is a little more tricky. Once you become skilled at performing, it becomes automatic. In contrast, problem solving requires thinking.

When doing a word or story problem in math or discussing a current event in history, you analyze facts and come to conclusions. Even when you've practiced a great deal and can think quickly, you still handle problem solving by thinking critically. Examples of problem solving include:

Working word problems
    in math
Debating an issue in
    current events
Analyzing an experiment
    in science
Identifying plants and animals
Explaining a poem

Knowing about the three types of practice allows you to choose the most effective practice for each course. In math, for instance, there are things to memorize, such as:

Names of geometric shapes,
    such as triangle, rhombus,
    parallelogram
Formulas for the area of a
    circle and the area
    of a triangle
Rules for simplifying equations

Just memorizing certain formulas can get you into trouble. Some formulas are similar and are easily misused. Using them correctly calls for understanding when and how they apply. For example:

Distance equals rate
    multiplied by time.
Time equals distance
    divided by rate.
Interest equals principal
    multiplied by rate
    multiplied by time.
Rate equals interest divided
    by principal and time.

WORKBOOK
PRACTICE 3-2

# Practice for Tests

Tests in school are a sort of competition. To do well in a contest, athletes get in shape. To train for a test in school, practice on the same types of questions or problems that will be on the test. Your assignments will usually provide that kind of practice, but not always.

Sometimes the homework assignment is different from the test. For example, your teacher may assign reading, but on the test you will have to answer questions. To do well on the test, read the assignment and then practice answering questions about it. Practicing what the test will ask you to do is especially effective.

Chapter 5 has more tips for doing well on tests.

# Choose a Place...

CONSISTENTLY DOING homework in a quiet, orderly place sets the stage for success. You can create the studio of a great homework artist. When you enter this place, your body and mind get the message: Time to get some work done. If you try to do homework in front of the TV, you get a different message: Time to be entertained. Distractions interfere with learning. Choose a **workplace** where studying does not compete for your attention. Your brain will thank you.

Even if you do some homework during study periods at school or at the library, you'll need a regular place to work at home. You'll also need a place to store your books and supplies. If you work at the kitchen or dining room table, you'll probably still store your things somewhere else and bring them out when you work. All it takes is a box or plastic crate that holds your supplies and is easy to carry.

Other supplies and equipment are listed below.

3x5 index cards
Watch
Calculator
Calendar
Dictionary
Thesaurus
Loose-leaf binder
Pens and pencils
Pencil sharpener
Eraser
Highlighters
Ruler
Tape
Stapler and staples
Paper clips
Rubber bands
Scissors
Three-hole punch

A N EFFECTIVE STUDY SPACE calls for a few essentials. One is a large table or desk that has enough room for you to spread out papers and books. A comfortable chair and good lighting are also helpful.

If you want to stay **organized**, use a file folder for each subject. Keep the file folders in a file drawer in a desk or in a box. The papers you save to study before tests, such as old tests and homework assignments, can go in your file folders at home.

WORKBOOK
JOURNAL 3-3

# ...and Equip Your Space

# Use a Three-Ring Binder

USING THREE-RING BINDERS is a handy, flexible way to organize handouts, notes, homework assignments, and tests. Stock a three-ring binder with the tools of the trade, and you'll be ready for masterful practice.

Start with a binder large enough for all the things you need in class on a regular basis, possibly one with two-inch rings. Try organizing your binder like the list to the right, and then change it to suit yourself.

Weekly schedule
To-Do List
Calendar

Divider for Subject #1
Master Plan
Assignment Sheets
Papers from this subject

Divider for Subject #2
Master Plan
Assignment Sheets
Papers from this subject

Divider for Subject #3
Master Plan
Assignment Sheets
Papers from this subject

Divider for Subject #4
Master Plan
Assignment Sheets
Papers from this subject

Extra notebook paper

*Follow this system for all your subjects. The forms on the following page can be found in Chapter 3 of* The Learning Power Workbook. *You have permission to copy these forms, and you may make as many copies as you need.*

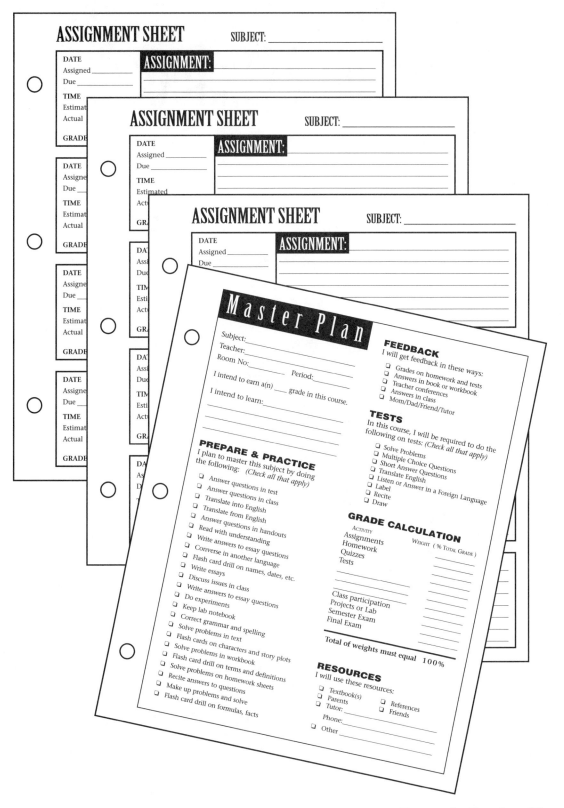

**ASSIGNMENT SHEET**     SUBJECT: _____

| DATE |  | **ASSIGNMENT:** |
| Assigned _____ | | _____ |
| Due _____ | | _____ |
| **TIME** | | _____ |
| Estimat | | |
| Actual | | |
| **GRADE** | | |

**ASSIGNMENT SHEET**     SUBJECT: _____

| DATE | **ASSIGNMENT:** |
| Assigned _____ | _____ |
| Due _____ | _____ |
| **TIME** | _____ |
| Estimated | |
| Act | |

**ASSIGNMENT SHEET**     SUBJECT: _____

| DATE | **ASSIGNMENT:** |
| Assigned _____ | _____ |
| Due _____ | _____ |

# Master Plan

Subject: _____
Teacher: _____
Room No: _____
_____ Period: _____
I intend to earn a(n) ___ grade in this course.
I intend to learn: _____
_____
_____

## PREPARE & PRACTICE
I plan to master this subject by doing the following: *(Check all that apply)*

❑ Answer questions in test
❑ Answer questions in class
❑ Translate into English
❑ Translate from English
❑ Answer questions in handouts
❑ Read with understanding
❑ Write answers to essay questions
❑ Converse in another language
❑ Flash card drill on names, dates, etc.
❑ Write essays
❑ Discuss issues in class
❑ Write answers to essay questions
❑ Do experiments
❑ Keep lab notebook
❑ Correct grammar and spelling
❑ Solve problems in text
❑ Flash cards on characters and story plots
❑ Solve problems in workbook
❑ Flash card drill on terms and definitions
❑ Solve problems on homework sheets
❑ Recite answers to questions
❑ Make up problems and solve
❑ Flash card drill on formulas, facts

## FEEDBACK
I will get feedback in these ways:

❑ Grades on homework and tests
❑ Answers in book or workbook
❑ Teacher conferences
❑ Answers in class
❑ Mom/Dad/Friend/Tutor

## TESTS
In this course, I will be required to do the following on tests: *(Check all that apply)*

❑ Solve Problems
❑ Multiple Choice Questions
❑ Short Answer Questions
❑ Translate English
❑ Listen or Answer in a Foreign Language
❑ Label
❑ Recite
❑ Draw

## GRADE CALCULATION

| ACTIVITY | WEIGHT ( % TOTAL GRADE ) |
|---|---|
| Assignments | |
| Homework | |
| Quizzes | |
| Tests | |
| _____ | _____ |
| Class participation | |
| Projects or Lab | |
| Semester Exam | |
| Final Exam | |

Total of weights must equal **100%**

## RESOURCES
I will use these resources:

❑ Textbook(s)
❑ Parents          ❑ References
❑ Tutor: _____   ❑ Friends
    Phone: _____
❑ Other _____

# Record Your Assignments

**M**ASTERING YOUR assignments begins with writing them down. Many students can tell horror stories about chapters they forgot to read or papers they forgot to write. Get your assignments down on paper, check them often, and you can erase that fear from your life.

To **record an assignment**, just fill in these items:

Date Assigned
Date Due
Assignment (exact description)

Also, list any required or recommended resources, such as magazines or library books. Here's how you might record a typical assignment.

---

## ASSIGNMENT SHEET          SUBJECT: _History_

| DATE | ASSIGNMENT: |
|------|-------------|
| Assigned _10/7_ | |
| Due _10/8_ | Read Chapter 4 |
| **TIME** | Write answers to Questions 2, 3, 4. |
| Estimated _2 hrs._ | Look up Kaiser Willhelm in the school library. |
| Actual _2 1/2 hrs._ | |
| **GRADE** _____ | |

| DATE | ASSIGNMENT: |
|------|-------------|

WORKBOOK PRACTICE 3-4   WORKBOOK PRACTICE 3-5

# Master Your Assignments

**Y**OU'VE RECORDED the assignment. Now is the time to get it done! Remember the **four steps to mastery**:

1. Plan
2. Prepare
3. Practice to mastery
4. Get prompt feedback

## STEP 1: PLAN

Take a few minutes to plan when and how to do the assignment. Planning means choosing the kinds of preparations, practice, and feedback that are most effective. What's more, planning helps you get started without procrastinating.

You may have time to do your planning in class when you get the assignment. If not, do it before the end of the school day. That way, things you may not have written down will still be fresh in your mind.

If you are unclear about the assignment, ask the teacher or a classmate for the missing information. Determine the books and papers you'll need to take home, and estimate how long the assignment will take. Then decide how to use your time. Your plan to master an assignment might involve the following:

PREPARING TO PRACTICE:
Read the chapter
Make flash cards
Refine lecture notes

PRACTICING:
Solve problems
Drill with flash cards
Answer questions at the
end of a chapter

GETTING FEEDBACK:
Go over the assignment in class
Ask your mom to check your work
Ask your brother to test you
Check answers in the back
of the book
Go to a study group
Answer quiz questions

## STEP 2: PREPARE

The material you will use for practice may be your notes from class, the text, some other book, or a handout. When you understand the information well enough to begin practice, your preparation is complete.

## STEP 3: PRACTICE TO MASTERY

Practice usually involves producing something on paper: writing an essay, solving problems, or answering questions at the end of a chapter. Some assignments may not call for you to hand in anything.

Suppose the assignment is to memorize the definitions of twenty new vocabulary words. You'll know that you've mastered these words when you can recite their definitions from memory. To prepare, you can make flash cards, writing each word on the front of a card and the definition on the back. To practice, test yourself by looking at each card and reciting the definition. If you are unsure, turn the card over for a reminder. Keep practicing until you master all twenty.

Mastery means that you can do whatever your assignment requires, accurately and quickly. You can demonstrate your skill or knowledge to anyone who might ask, and do it fast enough to succeed on tests.

Just finishing an assignment may not produce mastery. You may need more practice. You might answer the same questions or problems again, or you may be able to find more questions in your book. You may need to make up your own questions. This takes extra time, but mastery speeds up your learning rate, so you'll soon be saving time on later assignments.

If you get stuck, ask for help from Mom, Dad, a friend, or your teacher. After you get help, continue practicing to mastery. For instance, your assignment may be to complete ten algebra problems. You can do seven of them, but you need help with the last three. This means you haven't mastered that type of problem. Keep doing them, even problems that aren't in the assignment, until you can do that type easily.

## STEP 4: GET PROMPT FEEDBACK

It's best to get immediate feedback about your practice. That way you'll know if you've mastered the assignment or if you need more practice. As you gain experience, you'll learn to recognize when you have achieved mastery.

Ask your parent, tutor, or friend to tell you what you've done well and what needs improvement. The most useful feedback is free of scolding and insults. A baseball umpire demonstrates this when giving feedback to a pitcher. She doesn't coach, teach, praise, or criticize. She just says "Strike!" or "Ball!"

That's the kind of feedback needed for mastery learning. You just want to know if your work is on track or off, without shame or blame. The umpire doesn't say, "Who taught you to pitch?" or "Don't give up your day job."

Once you have mastered the assignment, write down the actual number of minutes or hours it took you on your Assignment Sheet. That will help you get better at planning and managing your time. When you have finished the assignment, cross it off your Assignment Sheet and pause to savor the feeling of accomplishment.

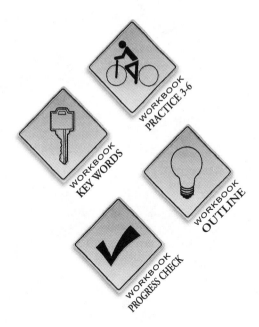

# Chapter 4 Objectives

After mastering this chapter you will be able to:

- USE PRQT, SQ3R, AND OTHER READING STRATEGIES

- TAKE NOTES USING THREE DIFFERENT METHODS

- IMPROVE YOUR MEMORY

- QUOTE A PASSAGE FROM SHAKESPEARE

# CHAPTER 4 READ, TAKE NOTE, AND REMEMBER

# Apply PRQT

ITH WONDERFUL intentions Marcus settles down with his history book. He realizes, after reading the first page, that he has comprehended nothing. Still, he trudges on through page two. His mind drifts to a CD that he wants to buy. Strains of music are now competing with history, and history is losing.

By page three the music has triggered daydreams of the game this weekend and hanging out with his friends. On page four Marcus is very relaxed. He can't sit up straight. He plops down on the bed with the book next to his head. Page five and Marcus is out for the count. History is history.

Marcus thinks he is a lousy reader because he has trouble concentrating. Learning history seems impossible, and he feels stupid. You may sometimes feel this way, too. The odds are that you have ample intelligence to be an excellent reader.

Get acquainted with a powerful reading method called **PRQT**. It is a technique that can help you pull the author's main points right off the page. PRQT stands for Preview, Read, Question, and Test.

## PREVIEW

Begin by looking over your reading assignment. Get a sense of what it's about, how it's organized, where it's going, and how long it is. Read the first paragraph or first page. Read the last paragraph or last page. If there is a summary, read that. Scan charts, tables, and pictures.

Read headings and titles. These often appear in **bold type**, *italics,* or ALL CAPITAL LETTERS. They may be underlined. Headings make your reading job easier. They break up long sections of text and signal that a new topic is coming up. Some authors pack the headings with their key terms and main points. If there are no headings, read the first sentence of each paragraph.

If there are questions at the end of the chapter or if your teacher gave you a handout for the reading assignment, read those during your preview. These questions reveal what your teacher and the author of the book intend for you to retain as you read.

## READ AND QUESTION

Read one paragraph at a time. Then, on a 3x5 card, write at least one question about that paragraph. Turn the card over and write the answer to your question. On the answer side, in the upper left corner, jot the page number and paragraph number so you will know where the information came from. The first paragraph on each page is #1, the second is #2, and so on.

page 148
paragraph 2

A substance is soluble if it disappears in the solvent (dissolves completely).

Some paragraphs have enough information for two or more questions. If so, use one card for each question and answer.

Reading this way takes effort and energy! Reward yourself for the work you're doing. Take a five-minute break after every twenty minutes of reading.

## TEST

Now test yourself using your question and answer cards. When you answer a question correctly, put that card in a pile to your right. Put those you miss in a pile to your left.

Keep working through the cards until they're all on your right. Then shuffle the stack and go through it again. Continue until you have mastered these questions. Congratulations! You've mastered your reading assignment.

PRQT offers some great advantages:

1. You learn more.

2. Practicing with flash cards, instead of re-reading the chapters, makes studying for tests faster and much easier.

3. Learning takes less time overall, even though PRQT takes more time than just reading an assignment straight through.

4. PRQT is less confusing than other reading techniques.

# Exercise

*Use PRQT to read an assignment for one of your other courses, or practice PRQT on a chapter that you've already read in one of your textbooks.*

*To help your memory, list the PRQT steps, along with a short description of each step, on a 3x5 card. Use it as a bookmark.*

# Experiment with Variations

**P**RQT works very well, and you might decide to use it just the way it is. It also comes with many variations. Following are some ways to modify PRQT.

## 1. Turn Headings into Questions

One alternative method is to write your questions before you read. To do this, turn headings into questions. Just reword them slightly. "Consequences of the Dred Scott Decision" becomes "What were the consequences of the Dred Scott Decision?"

## 2. Use PQRST
This adds a step to PQRT:

P — PREVIEW
Q — QUESTION
R — READ
S — SUMMARIZE
T — TEST

To use PQRST, preview the assignment and write down your questions before you start reading. Then, as you read each paragraph or section, take notes summarizing what you just read. When you finish reading and summarizing, test yourself with your questions.

## 3. Try SQ3R
SQ3R (called S-Q-Three-R) stands for:

S —SURVEY (Same as Preview)
Q—QUESTION
R—READ
R—RECITE (Summarize out loud)
R—REVIEW

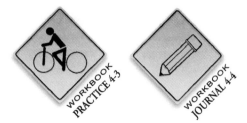

WORKBOOK PRACTICE 4-3

WORKBOOK JOURNAL 4-4

# Measure Your Reading Rate

Luckily, slow readers can probably double their reading rate with just a few hours of practice. As slow readers practice reading faster, they often understand and remember more. Faster reading not only saves you time, it also helps you learn more.

If your usual speed is below 200 words a minute, consider using the suggestions explained later in this chapter for increasing your reading skills. With those exercises you might learn to read 400 words a minute, or faster, in just a few hours.

READING RATE refers to how many words per minute you can read. This rate will vary with the material you are reading. It also depends upon how thoroughly you read to gain the information you need from a particular book or article. Most likely your reading rate for ordinary material is fairly stable.

Without actually knowing their reading rate, many people consider themselves slow readers. Rather than guessing you might as well find out. If your own reading rate is slow, your school assignments may take too much time.

# Increase Your Reading Skill

H ERE ARE SOME ways
to increase your
reading comprehension
and speed:

Be a flexible reader
Use a finger to pace your reading
Read, then reread faster
Build your vocabulary

## BE A FLEXIBLE READER

Your purpose for reading affects how fast you read and how much you try to remember. It is sometimes important to remember facts and details when you read. At other times, only the major points may interest you. When you entertain yourself by reading a detective story, you may not care if you remember any of it.

To zoom in on key facts or details, skim along quickly, looking only for the information you need. Don't read every word, or even every line. You may often find the information you want in lists, tables, or illustrations.

Sometimes it is necessary to read every word. You may need to read particularly complex material aloud. Lawyers often read aloud, word for word, to understand the language of a contract.

As a student you are expected to master complex ideas and remember many facts from textbooks. Reading slowly and deliberately may be the best way to acquire understanding.

## USE FINGER PACING

Pacing your reading with your finger can increase your reading speed and comprehension. Move your finger along each line as you read, and read at the pace your finger is moving.

To increase your reading speed, move your finger faster. Finger pacing does three things to increase reading speed:

1. It helps break the habit of going back to reread words and sentences that you understood the first time. (But if you really don't understand something on the first reading, then it is useful to read it a second time.)

2. It assists you to see more than one word at a time. This engages your peripheral vision, so you begin to see several words at a time.

3. Finger pacing encourages you to read faster. As your speed increases, you're likely to begin saying groups of words to yourself as you read. As you learn to read faster, your ability to concentrate will probably improve. That may explain why learning to read faster can lead to greater comprehension.

## READ, THEN REREAD FASTER

Learning to read faster takes practice. At first, you may not understand everything you read. You may also feel that you are missing important information.

Start by reading something that you already know. Read a page slowly enough to feel comfortable with your comprehension. Then, read the same page at a faster rate.

# Exercise

*To begin practicing finger pacing, turn this book upside down. Run your finger under each line, moving your finger smoothly and quickly from left to right. At the end of each line, jump your finger back to the left side of the next line.*

*As you do this exercise, move your eyes along with your finger. Since the book is upside down, you won't be reading. You are just practicing pacing your eyes with your finger. Do this exercise for one whole page in this book.*

## BUILD YOUR VOCABULARY

Here's a simple, effective way to practice new words you encounter while reading. When you come to a word you don't understand, write it on a 3x5 card and look it up in the dictionary. Then write its definition on the back of the card.

To bring new words into your long-term memory, use your vocabulary flash cards in three ways:

1. Look at the word and say the definition.
2. Look at the definition and say the word.
3. Look at the word and use it in a sentence.

As with any other memory work, drill until you know the words, then review from time to time.

# Exercise

*Choose a few pages of a book for practicing the read, then reread faster method. This strategy works well with novels or history books. It isn't recommended for math and science books.*

*Begin by reading a couple of pages twice. The first time, use finger pacing, but read slowly enough to comprehend it. When you have finished, read the same article a second time. Again use finger pacing, but this time go at a faster rate.*

*Don't expect sudden improvement after one practice. Just continue using this method, combining it with finger pacing. If you practice this way even a few times, your reading rate might increase so that your first—and perhaps only—reading of assignments can be faster.*

# Use Main Ideas & Supporting Facts

TAKING NOTES HELPS to keep your attention focused. Even better, you have the important points of the lecture recorded for later review. If you try to write down everything said during a lecture, you will probably fall behind and miss something. Many successful students take fewer notes rather than more.

The main ideas & supporting facts method works for almost any course.

Divide your note paper with a vertical line. Label the left half "Main Ideas." Label the right half "Supporting Facts."

Listen for the main ideas. Briefly note these on the left side of the paper. Expect only two or three main ideas in a one-hour lecture.

On the right side, jot down supporting facts, especially if you suspect they are not in the textbook. Supporting facts are those that support the main idea.

Keep your notes brief. There's no need to write a complete script of the lecture or capture all the details; that's what the textbook is for. Do note any facts about assignments and tests.

Study your notes for a few minutes as soon as possible after class. If you didn't note a main idea, add it now. You may also want to expand or edit your notes so they make sense when you study them later.

Use the main ideas & supporting facts method to take notes in several classes.

| MAIN IDEAS Author | SUPPORTING FACTS |
|---|---|
| Sir Arthur Conan Doyle | -lived 1859-1930<br>-creator of Holmes<br>-medical doctor<br>-wrote 56 short stories & 4 novels |
| Sherlock Holmes | -1887 to 1927<br>-detective character<br>-in over 100 films beginning in 1903<br>-"lived" at 221 B Baker St., London |
| Hound of the Baskervilles | -written in 1902<br>-considered Conan Doyle's masterpiece<br>-reason vs. superstition<br>-good vs. evil<br>-settings realistic |

WORKBOOK
PRACTICE 4-7

# Outline It

I T IS DIFFICULT to make a neat and accurate **outline** while listening to a lecture. However, after you read a chapter or study your notes from a lecture, creating a new, well-organized outline can help you digest and remember the information.

An outline is a list of main ideas with details and supporting facts listed under each main idea. Main ideas start at the left margin of the paper. Indent supporting facts under the main idea. You may use several levels of indenting to show more and more detail on any point.

Items in an outline are usually numbered, often with the main ideas in Roman numerals (I, II, III, IV). The next level down uses capital letters (A, B, C). Next come Arabic numbers (1, 2, 3) and then lower case letters (a, b, c).

WORKBOOK PRACTICE 4-8

MASS EXTINCTION—
65,000,000 YEARS AGO

I. What was affected?
   A. 38% of all marine animals
      1. reptiles
      2. fish
      3. sponges
      4. snails
      5. clams
      6. sea urchins
   B. Land animals
      1. dinosaurs
      2. reptiles
      3. mammals
      4. amphibians
   C. Land plants
      1. evidence in fossil pollen
         a. before extinction, mostly flower pollen and 25% fern pollen
         b. after extinction, 99% fern pollen

II. Explanations for extinction
   A. Global cooling
   B. Cosmic collision
      1. unusual pattern in rock layers
      2. high concentration of iridium (rare earth element)
      3. clouds of debris block sunlight
      4. fires
      5. release of poisons in water and air
   C. Volcanoes
      1. several erupted at same time
      2. flood volcanism
         a. high quantity of lava
         b. increases Earth surface temperature

# Make a Mind Map

A MIND MAP STARTS with the main idea written in the center of the page. Supporting ideas and facts stretch out in all directions from the center. Depending upon how much detail you are including, each supporting idea may have sub-ideas (like a tree whose branches divide into smaller and smaller branches until you get to the twigs).

When you Mind Map, you create a picture with your notes. The picture helps you remember key information. You can use colors, pictures, and symbols to designate themes, related ideas, and possible test questions. You may remember a point by visualizing it in the lower left corner of your Mind Map. Or, you may see it highlighted in green. It doesn't matter. Just seeing it helps you to recreate it.

As with outlining, Mind Mapping is not an activity to complete while listening to a lecture. Revise and add to your Mind Map after the lecture.

WORKBOOK
PRACTICE 4-9

WORKBOOK
JOURNAL 4-10

# Exercise

*Use the main ideas & supporting*
*facts method to take notes in a lecture.*
*After the lecture, reorganize and*
*complete your notes.*

*Use the outlining method to*
*take notes. After the lecture,*
*rewrite your outline.*

*Try Mind Mapping to take notes.*
*After the lecture, redraw your Mind*
*Map to include all the details you*
*wish to remember.*

# Remember

**W**HEN YOU LOOK up a phone number and then dial the number correctly, you use your short-term memory. If you just read the number aloud, even four or five times, you may not remember it a week later. That's because the phone number hasn't made it into your long-term memory. Putting things in long-term memory calls for special methods, described in the following articles.

Some people believe that human brains are like camcorders, recording every sight, sound, smell, taste, and feeling. Whether or not you accept this theory, you can pretend that it's true. Send yourself positive messages about your ability to remember, and your brain just might respond in kind.

Often you don't have to do anything special to store things in memory or pull them out again. When watching a movie, you store information—images and sounds in your mind. A friend then asks you about the show, and you recall it effortlessly and in great detail. Movies are easy to remember because they bombard your senses with vivid sights and sounds and involve your emotions with an engaging story. Remembering what happened in class usually isn't that easy. Skillful learning requires action.

Better grades, stronger skills, and more fun in school are the rewards of unlocking your long-term memory. Use the following **memory techniques** to claim your rewards.

Review
Use association
Picture it
Make flash cards
Try other methods

WORKBOOK
JOURNAL 4-11

# Review Review Review Review

SUPPOSE IT TAKES you ten repetitions to learn the words to a new song. Repeat the song fifteen times today, and you may remember more of it next week than if you only repeated it ten times.

Reviewing over time is often more efficient. First, memorize the song by looking and reciting until you have mastered all the words. Follow that with a five- or ten-minute break. Review again until you have the song mastered. Repeat the process within twenty-four hours. If you want to remember the song for a long time, review it again in a week and once more in a month.

You may be surprised at how well this method works. Reviewing soon after learning and again the next day can be far more efficient than putting in the same amount of work all at once.

To experience the benefit of review, apply the following steps.

1. Complete the initial learning. *(Practice to mastery for twenty to forty minutes. Break for five to ten minutes. Do your first review for five to ten minutes.)*
2. Review the next day. *(Practice to mastery for three minutes.)*
3. Review next week. *(Practice to mastery for two minutes.)*
4. Review next month. *(Practice to mastery for two minutes.)*

The time needed for mastery will vary with the length of the material you are memorizing. Experiment with different review schedules to learn what works for you.

Review your notes as soon as possible to begin moving information into your long-term memory. The simple act of reading your notes helps. To gain even more benefits, try these types of practice:

Revise your notes. Expand and edit. Reorganize and rewrite. Go for the level of detail you need.

Make flash cards and quiz yourself. Write key terms or questions on one side of the card. List definitions and answers on the back.

Regardless of the form of your class notes, convert them into a different format: main ideas & supporting facts, outline, or Mind Map.

# Exercise

*A little time has passed since you memorized the six components of a successful mindset ("Check Your Mindset" in Chapter 1). Review them now. Test yourself, starting with number one. Master one sentence before adding the next. Review again within twenty-four hours.*

# Use Association

REPETITION AND REVIEW are powerful ways to store information in your long-term memory. Adding another technique—association—can make memorizing easier and more fun. Following are some ways to use association. Experiment until you find the techniques that work best for you.

## CONNECT IT TO YOUR INTERESTS

We tend to remember that which interests us. If the subject you're learning isn't interesting, then search for an interesting connection. For example, you might think of the development of jazz and rock music as an aspect of American history. If you love cars, you can make connections with many principles in the field of science.

## GO FOR UNDERSTANDING

It's easier to remember something that you understand. Today's baseball scores are more readily remembered by sports fans than by someone who doesn't know the difference between home base and a home run.

Before you start to memorize something, do whatever it takes for you to understand it. Read additional information. Talk to another student. See your teacher. Ask a parent or family member to explain what it's about. Go for the big picture. Understand rules before exceptions. Organize the work by outlining or drawing a Mind Map. Understanding is especially important in math and science, where it's easy to confuse formulas and how to apply them.

## Use Mnemonics

Pronounce this word "nemoniks." A **mnemonic** is a play on words that helps you to remember something. The following jingles offer examples: Thirty days hath September, April, June and November. All the rest have thirty-one, save February, which has twenty-eight in fine—and leap year brings it twenty-nine. Put "i" before "e" except after "c," or when sounded like "a" as in "neighbor" or "weigh." You can make up your own mnemonic poems, raps, or jingles.

## Use Acronyms

An **acronym** is a word formed by the first letters in a series of other words. For example, NASA is an acronym for the National Aeronautics and Space Administration. Another acronym is the word HOMES, used to remember the names of the Great Lakes: Huron, Ontario, Michigan, Erie, Superior. Again, there's no need to stick with the old standbys. You can create your own acronyms.

## Set a Memory Trap

Say that it's Monday and you want to remember to call your aunt on Tuesday. Tie a string around your little finger. At the same time, make a mental note: "Tomorrow, when I see this string on my finger, I will remember to call my aunt."

During Tuesday morning's shower, you notice the string on your finger. "Oh yeah," you say to yourself, "as soon as I'm dry, I'll call Aunt Kim."

There are hundreds of other ways to set memory traps. Instead of tying a string to your finger, put a reminder in your pocket or switch your watch to the other wrist. Slip a rubber band around your wrist. Move a ring to a different finger. Set an alarm as a cue to do something.

# Make Flash Cards

**F**LASH CARDS engage all the elements of mastery learning, including preparation, practice, and feedback. They can make reviewing and preparing for exams a snap. Creating flash cards can save hours of study time.

Flash cards are particularly useful when you have to learn facts such as:

Names, dates, events in history
Meanings of words
Scientific facts and theories
Vocabularies in English or
    foreign languages
Mathematical formulas and facts
Rules of grammar

Here's a system for using flash cards:

1. Write a name, event, date, place, word, or question on the front of a 3x5 card. Then write the description, definition, explanation, or answer on the back side.

2. Practice with the cards, looking at the back side to check yourself or remind yourself of an answer you don't remember. Work with six to twenty cards at a time. Practice until you get most items right.

3. Next, set the cards you answer correctly in a pile to the right. Put those you miss in a pile to the left. Work with the cards on the left until you can add them to your right-hand pile.

4. Test your mastery by shuffling the deck and going through it again. If you miss any, put them to the left and repeat the process until you have mastered the whole deck.

5. Work with no more than twenty-five flash cards at a time. Master the first twenty-five, then the second twenty-five. Then combine them and master all fifty combined before adding any more.

6. Review your cards the next day and again in a week. Test yourself on the whole set. Set aside any you get wrong and go over those several times. Then, if you have time, test yourself again on the whole set.

7. You might try using different colors of 3x5 cards for different topics.

Some tasks require flash card alternatives or modified procedures:

Spelling
Sketching and labeling diagrams
Putting items in an order list

## SPELLING

When you look at a word on a flash card, you see the "answer" right away. That is, you see how to spell the word. Instead, get a friend or relative to go through the flash cards and quiz you. If no one is available, record the words using a tape recorder. Then test yourself by playing back the words and spelling them, one at a time.

You can also put the definition of the word on one side of the card and practice spelling the word when you see that.

## SKETCH AND LABEL DIAGRAMS

In some courses you might have to draw a map and label cities, rivers, and other features. In science courses you may learn the names of parts of plants and animals. These tasks are different from memorizing dates or definitions, since your learning is tied to a diagram. Here it makes sense to practice directly with the chart or diagram instead of a flash card.

If your teacher gives you a handout with space to label parts of something, make photocopies so you can use them when you review for tests. Making copies might be easier than creating flash cards.

If you want, you can still use flash cards for these tasks. On one side of the card write, "Make a sketch of a typical flower and label the parts." On the other side, do your sketch and label it.

## ORDERED LISTS

Sometimes the order of a series of facts or ideas is important. For example, you might learn the names of the last ten U.S. presidents or the order in which the original thirteen colonies ratified the U.S. Constitution. For a science class you may have to memorize the components of air in the order of their percentages of the total.

When using flash cards to learn such items, find a way to indicate their proper order. You could write the items you want to memorize on one side of the flash cards, and write the numbers on the backs. Practice by looking at the number sides.

Another way to remember ordered lists is to use the first letter of each item to create a nonsense phrase. For example, *My Dear Aunt Sally* is a way to remember the order of operations in solving algebraic equations (multiply, divide, add, and subtract).

WORKBOOK PRACTICE 4-12

# Picture It

PICTURING IS a powerful way to learn and remember. Verbal information is processed by parts of the brain that work with logic, numbers, and words. Other parts of the brain store images and recognize patterns. Forming pictures to go with the words will bring more of your brain power to memorizing words and information.

Certain subjects—such as geography, literature, and science—lend themselves well to mental pictures. Say you're reading the Autobiography of Malcolm X. Imagine being in the Norfolk Prison Colony where Malcolm X sits in the library. He is seeking to improve his vocabulary by copying the entire dictionary one word at a time. As you study the provinces of Canada, imagine being on the wind-swept prairie of Saskatchewan or in the snowcapped mountains of British Columbia.

Sometimes, an image may not readily come to mind. Let's say you are reading about the importance of private property in capitalism. Be creative, and remember that the picture doesn't have to make sense. You might think of Monopoly®, a real estate trading game. See Rich Uncle Pennybags as he walks down the street, clutching hotels and houses—a real estate tycoon holding his private property. You probably employ mental pictures already. Think of a state on the west coast of the United States. Now think of one on the east coast, and now a state near the middle of the country. You probably have a picture of a map of the United States in your mind. This is an example of using pictures as a memory aid.

# Try More Memory Methods

### LOOK/LOOK AWAY

When you want to memorize written material, look at it, then look somewhere else and recite it. If you get stuck, glance down for a reminder. Then look up and recite again. This is called the look/look away method.

### WALK AROUND

It helps to move your body while memorizing. Many people find it easier to memorize while walking. If you are working at home, experiment with pacing in your room or walking around the block as you memorize.

### MASTER IT WORD FOR WORD

To memorize something word for word, master one phrase or sentence at a time. Completely master the first portion before working on the second. Mastery means you can say it without straining or stumbling—as confidently as you can spell your own name. After you master the second sentence, master the first and second sentences together before working on the third. Continue in this way until you have memorized the material.

## Exercise

*The techniques discussed in this chapter are listed below. Create a set of flash cards to help you remember them.*

*PRQT        PQRST*
*SQ3R        Mind Mapping*
*Main ideas & supporting facts*
*Outlining    Look/Look away*
*Walking Around   Picturing*
*Word for Word Mastery*
*Association        Flash cards*

*Write the name of each technique on a single card. On the back describe the technique and give one or more examples of how to use it. Practice with your flash cards until you feel sure you will remember the methods. Tomorrow review your flash cards again.*

WORKBOOK PRACTICE 4-13

# Exercise

## QUOTE SHAKESPEARE

The final exercise is to memorize half or all of a 200-word passage from William Shakespeare, using techniques from this chapter. Using these tools, you may find that you can master this assignment in less than one hour. Aim to get every word exactly right and to recite the whole piece without stumbling or pausing to think.

Here are some suggestions:

• Read the whole passage. Several unusual words are defined at the end of the passage. Look up any other words you don't know in a dictionary.

• Notice that the passage is organized based on the stages in life.

• Use the look/look away method to memorize one line at a time. Master the first two lines of the poem together before starting on line three. Continue through the rest of the passage in the same way.

• When you start to work on each sentence, create a picture to go with that sentence.

• Notice that as you learn the words, the poetry begins to make more sense.

When you finish memorizing, give this passage to someone else and ask that person to listen as you recite. Have that person check the accuracy of your delivery. Notice how it feels to master an assignment like this.

# A passage from As You Like It

*by William Shakespeare (This famous quotation is from a speech by Jacques.)*

All the world's a stage,
And all the men and women merely players.
They have their exits and their entrances;
And one man in his time plays many parts,
His acts being seven ages. At first the infant,
Mewling and puking in the nurse's arms.
Then the whining schoolboy, with his satchel,
And shining morning face, creeping like snail
Unwillingly to school. And then the lover,
Sighing like a furnace, with a woeful ballad
Made to his mistress' eyebrow. Then a soldier,
Full of strange oaths, and bearded like the pard,
Jealous in honor, sudden and quick in quarrel,
Seeking the bubble reputation
Even in the cannon's mouth.
And then the justice,
In fair round belly with good capon lined,
With eyes severe and beard of formal cut,
Full of wise saws and modern instances;
And so he plays his part. The sixth age shifts
Into the lean and slipper'd pantaloon,
With spectacles on nose and pouch on side;
His youthful hose, well sav'd, a world too wide
For his shrunk shank, and his big manly voice,
Turning again toward childish treble, pipes
And whistles in his sound. Last scene of all,
That ends this strange eventful history,
Is second childishness, and mere oblivion,
Sans teeth, sans eyes, sans taste, sans every thing.

---

**DEFINITIONS OF UNUSUAL WORDS**

capon: a neutered chicken
hose: long stockings
mewling: babbling
pard: a character in Chaucer's Canterbury Tales, who even as an adult man had only "peach fuzz" rather than a beard
sans: without
saws: sayings
shank: body or legs
woeful: sad

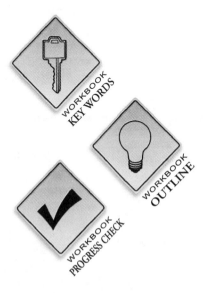

WORKBOOK KEY WORDS

WORKBOOK OUTLINE

WORKBOOK PROGRESS CHECK

# Chapter 5  Objectives

After mastering this chapter you will be able to:

- **PREPARE FOR AND TAKE TESTS MORE SUCCESSFULLY**

- **MANAGE STRESS BEFORE AND DURING TESTS**

- **KEEP GRADES IN PERSPECTIVE**

# CHAPTER 5 TESTS AND GRADES

# Prepare For Your Tests

THERE'S A TEST next week. You have a clear picture of what will be on it. You spend a little time reviewing, and you see that there are only a few things you haven't mastered. During the coming week, you learn them. Relaxed and confident, you take the test. There are no surprises. You work quickly, but carefully, never feeling rushed or stressed. A few days later your test paper is back, marked with an "A."

If it sounds like a dream, think again. This could really happen to you. To find out how, read on.

## GET CLUED-IN EARLY

You can start preparing for tests the first minute you walk into class at the beginning of the term. Many teachers will tell you right away about how they grade tests. Pay close attention and take notes.

## MASTER EVERY ASSIGNMENT

Master each assignment from day one. If you have a test approaching and you haven't practiced to mastery, there may still be time to master some or all of the material.

Remember that mastery learning helps you retain information longer and learn additional material faster. In many cases, the extra time you spend mastering every assignment will reduce the total hours needed to get the grade you want.

## MAKE YOUR OWN STUDY TOOLS

Creating flash cards, outlines, and Mind Maps helps you learn the information now, and these **study tools** will help you prepare for tests.

Before you start working on hand-outs that contain diagrams to label or exercises to complete, make a few copies of them. Use these copies as practice when you review for exams.

## DRILL AND REVIEW OFTEN

Move information from short-term to long-term memory by **reviewing** and studying several times over a period of days or weeks.

## SAVE OLD TESTS

Save your tests as you go along. This will help you prepare for the final. Another good reference would be old exams you might get from someone who took the course last year.

Some teachers use the same exams over and over. If so, they will generally collect all old tests. Talk with someone who had this teacher before. Their experiences and memories may be a great help to you.

## FIND OUT THE GROUND RULES

If you don't know vital information about a test, find out: "What materials can I use during the test?" "Is there a guessing penalty for wrong answers?" "What types of questions will be on the test?" "How many questions will there be?" "What information or chapters will it cover?" "How do you suggest I study?" "How will you grade?"

When grading essay tests, some teachers may subtract points for incorrect spelling and grammar. Others may grade only on the content and organization of your writing. Find out.

To prepare effectively, you may need more information about a test than your teacher has revealed.

## MEET WITH YOUR TEACHER

Most teachers will appreciate your extra effort to learn. Remembering this may help you feel more comfortable about asking your teacher to meet with you before or after school.

## MAKE AN EDUCATED GUESS

Even if you follow all the previous suggestions, you can never be certain what will be on the test. What you can do is make an educated guess. Here are two suggestions.

First, make a list of what you are expected to know. Plan how you will learn each topic and estimate the time that it will take. Make a schedule to do that learning and keep to it.

Second, write your own practice test using everything you know about the course, the teacher, and the upcoming exam. Make up questions from class notes, your textbook, handouts, and homework assignments.

## TEST YOURSELF

Football teams play practice games. This is called scrimmaging. The same idea can work for you. Scrimmage with your practice test, and set a time limit for completion.

If you know the material fairly well, you can test yourself before reviewing and studying. The practice test can help you zero in on the few things you need to brush up on. If you are not up-to-date in a course, study first, then take your practice test. Use it to spot any weak areas you'll want to strengthen.

## BE ACTIVE

There is a difference between study and practice. To practice is to be active. Practice doing the things you will be expected to do on the test. Answer questions, solve problems, draw diagrams, or write essays. You may need to prepare by reading the text or your notes or by making an outline or mind map to summarize the material. Don't stop there. Practice to mastery.

WORKBOOK
PRACTICE 5-1

# CRAM
## At Your Own Risk

**C**RAMMING IS STUDYING intensely right before a test. Cramming may help you pass the test, but two weeks later you probably won't remember much. That's because you didn't learn much.

Cramming ignores the principle of regular reviews to put information into long-term memory. Most people rapidly forget after they cram, so they don't build up their knowledge. That makes it much harder to learn new material, and passing the next test gets tougher.

Here are some pros and cons of cramming:

PROS:
> You have to study only for a day or two.
> You might pass the exam.

CONS:
> The time spent in class wasn't productive.
> You probably don't remember what you studied while cramming.
> You have a weak foundation for future learning.
> Not understanding the subject and forgetting information can be hard on your self-esteem.

If you do end up cramming, forgive yourself. Then begin practicing and reviewing to avoid cramming next time.

WORKBOOK
PRACTICE 5-2

# Ace That Test!

THERE IS MORE to taking tests than knowing your subject. Improve your score with techniques you can put to work before and during the test.

## COME WELL-STOCKED

Make a list of the things you want to have on hand during the test. Common items include textbooks, dictionaries, calculators, pencils, and erasers. To avoid added stress the morning of the test, gather these things the night before.

## WARM UP

Spend a few minutes reviewing before the test. This will warm up your brain circuits. Make a quick Mind Map or outline. If you have some flash cards, do a short drill. For a math or science test, solve a problem or two.

## ARRIVE EARLY

Arriving early gives you time to get settled and even use some of the relaxation techniques described later in this chapter.

## READ THE DIRECTIONS

Some executives in Minneapolis wanted to see if anyone was reading the literature their bank was mailing to customers. They sent out brochures that included a sentence that offered $50 to anyone who simply wrote and asked for it. They had no takers.

Your test directions probably won't include any cash offers, but often there are "free" points for the taking. Read directions carefully, and you'll find information that can make a real difference in your grade.

When students skip the directions or read them too quickly, they end up writing essays instead of short answers or answering four questions when the directions tell them to do three out of four. Avoid a similar fate by following directions.

## BUDGET YOUR TIME

Each test comes with a time limit. A question's worth is measured in points. To budget your time, the aim is to look at the point value of each question and give it the time and energy it's worth— no less, no more.

Concentrate on the questions that are worth the most points. Skip over questions that could take more time than they're worth.

Estimate the time for each question based on its point value. Typically there are 100 total points on a test. If you have fifty minutes, that means each point is worth one-half minute of your time. For a ten-point question, you would budget five minutes. For a twenty-point question, ten minutes.

If all the questions have the same point value, divide your time equally. Check the clock and manage your time accordingly.

## START WITH EASY QUESTIONS

Work the simplest problems or questions first. Easy questions will help you warm up and boost your confidence. Completing them quickly gives you time in the bank to spend later on the more difficult questions.

If you can't think of the answer to a question right away, pass it by for the moment. Reading the question has acted like a request to your subconscious mind. Leaving the question for later gives your mind time to deliver an answer.

## GUESS—UNLESS

Some tests have a guessing penalty, such as two points for a right answer and a half-point off for a wrong answer. If there is a penalty, guess only if you are fairly sure about the answer. Otherwise, skip the question. If there is no penalty for wrong answers, imagine that you know the answer and then guess.

## TAKE IT EASY

Pause at times during the test to relax. Breathe slowly and deeply. Notice your point of attention and bring it back to the present. Take one question at a time, and don't worry about the last question or the ones coming up. Let go of anxiety about your final score and simply do your best. Your fate in school or life doesn't hang on the way that any single test turns out.

## ADJUST YOUR TECHNIQUE TO THE TEST

Different kinds of tests call for different approaches. Following are some hints.

### Multiple Choice

Try to answer each question in your head before reading the possible answers.

Read all the possible answers before choosing one.

When in doubt, guess. Eliminate the choices that are obviously wrong. If you get stuck on two answers that are almost the same, just choose one and move on.

Go with your first impression about which answer is correct unless there's a compelling reason to change your mind.

Eliminate answers that form a sentence with incorrect grammar.

Watch for absolute words such as *always* and *never,* which often signal false statements.

### Short-Answer

Keep your answers brief to save time. These are not essay questions.

Focus on one key term, event, concept, or definition for each question.

Don't give the short-answer part of a test more time than it's worth. Often you can gain more points in essay or multiple-choice sections.

### Essay

Take a minute to make a quick outline. List the key points you want to make. Then number these points right on the test, according to the order you want them to appear in your final answer. Even if you don't finish an answer, you might get some points for having a clear outline.

Avoid "filler" sentences. Be brief. Get to the point.

Write neatly.

Pace yourself. Glance at the clock periodically to make sure you're allowing about the right amount of time for each question.

Read the questions carefully. Look for the key verbs that tell you how to answer:

*Analyze* means "break this topic into separate parts and explain each one."

*Compare* means "show how these things are similar and different."

*Contrast* means "explain how these things differ."

*Define* means "explain what this means."

*Evaluate* means "give your opinion about the quality or worth of this subject, and back your opinion with evidence."

*Illustrate* means "furnish examples of this topic."

*Summarize* means "list the main points."

### True-False

Read questions very carefully. The difference between a true statement and a false one is often a matter of one word.

Look for words such as *never* and *always*. Statements containing these words are often false.

Remember, if any part of a statement is false, the whole statement is false.

## REVIEW YOUR WORK

Even if you haven't answered all the questions, take a few minutes at the end of the period to check your work. Make sure your name is on each piece of paper, and number the pages and answers. Look over your work and make any last minute corrections.

WORKBOOK PRACTICE 5-3

WORKBOOK JOURNAL 5-4

# Beware of C-H-E-A-T-I-N-G

CHEATERS PAY A PRICE for whatever they gain. Sometimes that price is steep. The first cost is the missed opportunity to practice and to build a strong foundation for the learning that comes next. People who cheat are making a trade. They trade the possibility of a higher grade now for mastery of the subject.

Some cheaters hope that other people will think they are cool: "Look at me. I passed this test, and I didn't even have to study." The trouble is that everyone knows the truth. Cheating is born of failure, and the act of cheating is an admission of that failure.

When a student cheats off another, the cheater takes advantage of the other student's work. If the teacher grades on a curve, a cheater affects all of the other students.

Teachers may believe that the cheating student is ready to move to the next level. The student knows this isn't true. This can undermine the student's self-esteem.

Students who cheat give up independence and self-control. They are no longer thinking for themselves. They have given that job to someone else. They are dependent on someone else doing the practice, gaining the knowledge, and doing the thinking.

Students who cheat can isolate themselves. When they ask someone if they can copy homework, they can lose a friend. The other student can easily feel uncomfortable or taken advantage of. If word gets out that a student is cheating, more friends may be lost. People don't always trust someone who cheats.

There is also the matter of getting caught. That's a risk most students can live without.

Taking responsibility for your own accomplishments in school is a way to live your own life. Cheating compromises that goal.

WORKBOOK
JOURNAL 5-5

# Take the Feedback

## DON'T WORRY

When it's over, it's over. There is nothing to do about your answers. What you can do is decide where to place your attention. Focus on what you did well, and don't worry about what you might have gotten wrong. Think back to how you prepared for the test, or how you got there early, or how you budgeted your time during the test. Note these things in your Success Log.

## USE THE TEST AS FEEDBACK

Did you study the right stuff? Did you correctly anticipate the types of questions that were on the test? If so, take a bow. You're mastering a very useful skill.

What kinds of mistakes did you make? Did you misunderstand the directions? Do you disagree with your teacher's **assessment** of your answers? If so, ask him for time to talk about your test. Some teachers allow students to correct their exams and turn in the work for extra credit.

If there was something on the test that you haven't mastered, consider mastering it. It will probably be important in the rest of the course, and not knowing it could stop your progress. This may take self-discipline, but the payoff could be well worth the effort.

Give yourself credit for what you've learned. If you scored seventy-five percent, you learned a lot. You are probably closer to mastery than your grade may indicate.

# Handle the Stress

OME OF US have learned to fear tests. The key word is learned. If you learned your reaction to tests, then you can also learn a new way to respond to them.

Fear is not a monster to be avoided. It is a feeling. And like other feelings, fear consists of two basic things, thoughts and body sensations. Fear exists to serve us. It signals us to choose carefully and protects us from undesirable situations. Fear boosts our adrenaline, creating energy that can be channeled into productive use. (Some performers call this their competitive edge.)

Learn to explore your fears. Get to know each one fully. Accept it for the message it brings. If your fear serves no purpose, you can choose to move beyond it. Use the following process any time you're worrying about an upcoming test or assignment.

Imagine the worst that can happen:

*"I'll bomb this test so badly that I can never face my friends again. I'll flunk the course. I'll flunk out of school. I'll never get a job. I'll end up on the streets, begging for food, all because of this quiz!"*

Allow yourself to feel afraid and embarrassed about blowing the test. Focus your attention on the sensations in your body. Where is the fear located? Is it in your stomach? hands? legs? throat? Study each sensation. Describe it in words. As you describe the feelings, they will begin to fade away. Keep imagining your test nightmare and noticing the physical sensations. Do this until the emotional charge in your body is gone.

Next, let those worst possible outcomes drift away. Now begin to create a vivid picture of success:

*You enter the room early. You have everything you need. You take a few moments to imagine success. Your teacher hands you the test, and you read it over carefully. You know the answers and feel good about yourself. You see yourself writing calmly and confidently. You have time to review your answers before turning them in. A few days later the teacher returns your test paper. The grade you wanted is written in red at the top of the page. You feel triumphant.*

Just before the test, or even during the test, you can revisit your image of success. Zoom in to that scene and make it bright and colorful. Hold that positive picture as you work.

WORKBOOK
JOURNAL 5-7

# Exercise

*Tomorrow you will have an exam in a course that is difficult for you. Imagine your vivid picture of success.*

*Now imagine that it is the day of the test. Return to your image of success.*

# Trade In Those Negative Thoughts

**E**VEN WHEN you have the right equipment and do the right things, you may not be as successful as you want to be. Maybe your efforts to be successful are in a fight with your beliefs about what you can accomplish. If you keep saying to yourself that you're lousy in math, then you might be lousy in math no matter how hard you try. Tell yourself that you'll never make it to college, and you could sabotage your success in high school, even while you work hard in your courses.

Our achievements in life and how we feel about ourselves are connected to what we think is possible. Our thoughts and beliefs are very powerful.

They are invisible, but they are as powerful as what we do and what we have.

Positive thoughts and beliefs about who you are and who you can be will make a great difference in your life. When you have doubts about your abilities or feel frustrated and discouraged about certain subjects, trade in those negative thoughts.

Start by taking a good look at where you are now. Tell the truth. What do you really think about yourself? What do you tell yourself about who you are? Spend a little time dwelling on your answers to these questions. Consider writing them down or speaking them out loud. This can help put a little distance between you and your thoughts. What sounds sensible inside your head may sound silly when spoken out loud.

In some cases, you'll find that those thoughts and worries disappear when you really examine them. In other cases, you may discover that there is an overwhelming amount of evidence to contradict what you usually say to yourself.

Consider the student who tells himself that he is lazy because he sometimes doesn't finish his reading assignments. What he isn't taking into account is that he cooks dinner for his family three nights a week, baby-sits after school for two hours every day, participates in a youth group, and marches in the band. He is definitely not lazy.

When this student sits down to his homework at 10:00 p.m. and struggles to stay awake, he thinks there is something wrong with his ability to read. His problem is really one of time management. His harsh judgment of himself makes it hard for him to see that. He can replace his "I am lazy" with "I am ambitious, responsible, and capable of reading anything I want to read." This will allow him room to devise an effective time-planning strategy.

Imagining the results you want is a powerful strategy. Forming positive images will help you get mobilized to take effective action. After all, if you do what you've always done, you can expect the results you've always gotten. Different results require different actions.

Finally, take time to notice your accomplishments. Keeping a Success Log will focus your attention on your growing capabilities and help you build a positive reputation with yourself.

# Build a Portfolio

PORTFOLIOS ARE collections of samples or records of accomplishments. A school portfolio usually includes samples of a student's best work. Your portfolio shines a light on what you've done. It communicates what you want others to know about you.

Some teachers use portfolios as a substitute for grades. They believe that portfolios give a fuller, richer picture of their students than number or letter grades. Learning to develop portfolios may also serve you in the future.

A job application is a kind of portfolio—a listing of your experiences and accomplishments, designed to interest an employer. A resume and letters of recommendation round out this portfolio even more.

Teachers who assign portfolios will tell you what to include. Depending on the subject, you may collect term papers, test scores, art projects, sheet music, audiotapes or videotapes, computer printouts, or photographs.

A portfolio is like a three-dimensional autobiography. It tells a story about you, one with a beginning, middle, and end. Help your audience stay focused and interested in the "plot."

Following are some tips for creating an interesting and well-organized portfolio:

Know your purpose. Are you creating a portfolio to apply for a job? to meet the requirements for a course? to celebrate your personal accomplishments? to get to know yourself better? Your purpose dictates what your portfolio includes and how it's organized.

Know your audience. Think about their purpose for looking at your portfolio. What would they like to know about you? What does your audience already know about you? Create your portfolio to answer their major questions.

Guide your audience. A table of contents and an index, along with captions that describe each sample, help keep your audience from getting lost.

WORKBOOK PRACTICE 5-9

# Play the GrAde Game

GETTING GOOD GRADES may seem like a game at times, but it's an important game. How you play it can make a difference in your experience of school now and in your options for the future. Getting low grades is no fun and can be a hassle in your life. In addition, grades are one way to measure your skill at learning. That skill is important, no matter what you decide to do with your life.

Grades are important, but they are not the most important part of learning. "Grades are totally subjective," you might hear people say. It's true that standards differ from teacher to teacher. What passes for an "A" in one course might get only a "B" or a "C" in another.

Getting a high grade does not always mean that you understand the subject. Nor does studying for long hours guarantee good grades.

Figure out a way to make the grade game work for you. Get good grades at the same time you are learning what you need in order to achieve your own goals.

Give some thought to the notion: You are not your grades. You are far more than that. Grades don't measure much of what is important in life, such as your passions, your experiences, your talents, your dreams, what you do for others, or the love in your heart. A grade measures only one thing—your performance on an assignment, on a test, or in a course.

You are a complex being—alive, thinking, and feeling. So put your grades in perspective. Grades are a way to measure your current level of skill in one of life's games.

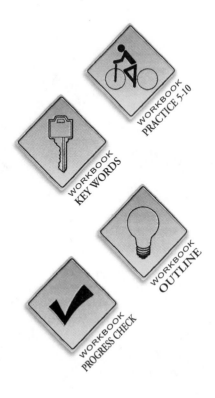

# Chapter 6 Objectives

After mastering this chapter you will be able to:

- COMMUNICATE MORE EFFECTIVELY

- USE I-MESSAGES IN EMOTIONAL SITUATIONS

- NEGOTIATE WIN-WIN AGREEMENTS

# CHAPTER 6 TALK IT OUT

# Speak Effectively

OST LIBRARIES have a whole shelf of books about relationships. The variety of recommendations they contain can make this subject seem very complicated. It often boils down to communication. In most relationships someone speaks, someone listens, and they try to reach agreements. Problems in relationships often start with ineffective communication.

You can stop conflict before it starts by getting back to the basics: speaking and listening. Suggestions for effective speaking follow. For ideas about listening, check out the next article.

## KNOW YOUR PURPOSE

We usually have a purpose for starting a conversation. We begin with a goal in mind, something that we want. When we know what we want and ask for it, we're more likely to achieve our goals. Our purpose may be as simple as obtaining a ride to school or as complex as resolving a bitter disagreement.

## NOTICE YOUR TONE

The way you emphasize words makes a huge difference in the messages you send. If you sound hostile, angry, or indifferent, many people will hear only your tone of voice—no matter what words you use. Their response to your speaking will probably be negative.

## MAKE REQUESTS

After deciding what you want, make a direct **request**. The advantages of doing so are many:

Requests help everyone involved know what we really want.

Requests give others freedom to say "yes" or "no."

Requests keep us focused on what we want today, right now, instead of on old arguments.

Requests help you to reach **agreements**. To understand how this works, practice changing complaints into requests. "You always interrupt me" becomes "Please give me a chance to talk." "This assignment to write a term paper is a waste of time" becomes "Can you help me understand the purpose of this paper?" When you make requests, you prevent problems and invite solutions.

## NOTICE YOUR BODY LANGUAGE

Your body sends messages twenty-four hours every day in a language all its own. **Body language** includes your **posture**, facial expression, clothes, **grooming**, and much more. What you don't put into words says a lot.

To speak clearly, keep the way you *look and move* in agreement with what you say. When your body language conflicts with your verbal language, you leave people confused. Notice your body language and the impact of your gestures. For example, watch how people react to the way you stand.

Make eye contact. Eyes say a lot. If you keep looking away or shifting your eyes, others might think you're bored or angry. You don't have to glare or stare like a zombie. Just look at people when you're speaking to them, especially into their eyes.

## USE I-MESSAGES

An I-message is especially effective in tense or emotional situations. I-messages accomplish two goals. They describe the experience you are having, and they communicate without blaming or judging the other person. At first, using them will probably feel awkward. With practice you will be able to state your thoughts, feelings, and desires clearly, without attacking or blaming others.

I-messages are made up of five parts. You don't have to include all five. Your observations, feelings, and wants are most important.

### 1) "I OBSERVE . . ."

Lead off with a statement of what you can see, hear, touch, taste, or smell. Others would observe the same things. This is *not* your judgment about the event or person. For example, "You make our room so messy" or "You are such a slob" are statements of judgment, not of what you observe. To put it purely in terms of what you observe, you might say, "I see clothes on the floor, the bed isn't made, and there are dirty dishes on my desk."

### 2) "I THINK . . ."

Here is your opportunity to briefly state your thoughts on the subject. It is important not to turn this into a you-message. "I think you are inconsiderate" is a you-message disguised as an I-message and will probably get you in an argument. "A messy room makes it hard to find things" is less likely to start a fight.

### 3) "I FEEL . . ."

This is where you share your emotional reactions to the situation. Use words to describe what you feel—happy, sad, frustrated, afraid, mad, uptight, giddy. People easily confuse their thoughts with their feelings. For example, "I feel that we should have a clean room" doesn't express a feeling. "I feel frustrated about sharing a room with you" does.

### 4) "I WANT . . ."

This step moves you in the direction of a request. "I want to find a way to live in this room together without driving each other crazy."

### 5) "I INTEND . . ."

Here you make your next step known to the other person. "I intend to work this out with you. Can we set up a time to talk about our room?"

Notice that the other person was not put down or blamed. He was invited to participate in a problem-solving exercise that could get both people more of what they want.

Statements that begin with the word *you* can easily be critical or blaming. "You make me angry by listening to my telephone conversations" is an example. Change this to an I-message: "I feel uncomfortable talking on the phone with my girlfriend while you are in the room."

You-message: "Why are you always eavesdropping on me?"

I-message: "I would like it if you would stay out of my room when I'm on the phone."

Remember, I-messages describe your experience without blaming or judging the other person;

"I feel happy when you make the bed."

"I see tears on your face."

"I'm thinking about your grade on the science test."

"I want you to leave me alone for a while."

"I plan to see a movie tonight."

I-messages don't work for everything we have to say, but they work well for inviting dialogue and cooperation. When you ask other people for something and they say no, use this I-message: "I'd really like to know more." It says that you are willing to listen and go deeper into their point of view. This I-message invites further conversation—more so than "Why not?" or "You always say no to me!"

The way you talk, including your tone of voice, body language, and specific phrases, affects the responses you get.

WORKBOOK
PRACTICE 6-1

# Listen Actively

LISTENING MIGHT sound simple, but it's not. Often our listening fails—especially during arguments and fights, when listening counts the most. We can usually tell when other people are really listening to us. It's easy to forget that *they* can also tell if we are listening to them. When we don't listen, other people can feel angry or hurt. They are then less likely to see our point of view or agree to what we want.

## EITHER LISTEN OR SPEAK

We have all been in arguments when everybody talked at once. Instead of listening, everyone tried to say their piece and get their own way. Communication totally broke down.

To avoid this situation, either listen *or* speak. Avoid mixing the two. It's easier to master these two skills when you practice them one at a time.

## ANNOUNCE YOUR INTENTION

At first, **active listening** might seem strange to you and others. Try announcing your intention:

"I don't want to fight about this. Let's try something else. I'll listen to you, and then I'll tell you what I heard. When you know that I really understand you, I'd like you to do the same for me.

## NOTICE WHEN QUESTIONS AREN'T QUESTIONS

Some questions are statements in disguise. "Do you really like that compact disk?" probably means "I hate what you're listening to." Similarly, "Why are you doing that?" might mean "Please stop it."

Ask direct questions when you genuinely lack information, ideas, or resources.

## SUM UP THE OTHER PERSON'S MESSAGE

Sometimes people will tell you what they're thinking and feeling. At other times, discovering how a person feels or what he thinks takes a lot of conversation. It works well to sum up another person's point of view before talking about yours. This is called active listening. Certain phrases come in handy:

"Oh, I see. What you think is . . ."
"What I'm hearing you say is . . ."
*"If I understand you correctly,* what you would like is . . ."

Ask other people to tell you when you have it right. When you understand the other person's point of view, say so:

**You:** Curtis, I feel ticked off when you're late, and you have been late three times this week.

**Curtis:** You are late a lot yourself.

**You:** You think you're on time as often as I am. Is that what you're saying?

**Curtis:** Yeah, that's right.

## SEPARATE LISTENING FROM AGREEING

Using active listening doesn't mean you agree. You can listen carefully to the other person and his feelings, even if you think he is wrong or unreasonable. Let him know that you hear him. If you still disagree, it's not due to lack of understanding or caring.

Whenever you listen, you can stay in charge of your response. You choose whether to agree with or act on the other person's message.

## KNOW WHEN TO FOCUS ON FEELINGS

Consider the following exchange:

**Tamika:** What a day! My dad was in a terrible mood, and then two teachers gave me a hard time. I have an awful headache.

**Richard:** So what are you doing to change all this?

It sounds like Tamika is upset and wants to talk about it. Richard's response assumes that she is interested in talking about how to fix the situation. Perhaps in a few minutes or a few days she will be, but maybe not now. Right now she probably wants Richard just to hear about her feelings. Solving problems can wait for later.

Richard's new response focuses on Tamika's feelings. He could say, "It sounds like you really had a bummer of a day. What happened?"

## GIVE IT TIME

When the topic is emotional or a continuing source of conflict, it may take several rounds of active listening to get everyone's cards on the table. Say that you're in a tense conversation with someone you really dislike. Consider doing a few hours of active listening with this person, possibly over several days, before you try to solve any problems.

## DECIDE HOW MUCH IS ENOUGH

Active listening is a useful tool, but not in every conversation. When communication is easy and businesslike, active listening techniques are inappropriate. Active listening is designed for times when people get angry, shout, mumble, or walk away.

Active listening also takes concentration. If you run out of energy or self-control, end the conversation and continue later.

Once others agree that you accurately understand them, you can state your case. Say what you think, including any disagreements you have with what you've just heard. Use I-messages.

Active listening can be time-consuming. It is worth the time and effort, especially when it resolves long-standing arguments and prevents new ones.

WORKBOOK PRACTICE 6-2

# Create Win-Win Agreements

I T IS COMMONLY ASSUMED that in order for one person to win, somebody else has to lose. This may not be true. Creating win-win agreements means solving problems in a way that works for everyone involved. Practice looking for the "win option," a new solution that helps everyone get what they want.

Sometimes, when you understand the other person's point of view, you might see that there is no problem or conflict. A simple agreement may get both of you what you want.

Sometimes there is a real difference of opinion. The other person feels that giving you what you want means giving in. You feel the same way about giving her what she wants. Finding a solution you can both live with will take work. Agreements with teachers and parents about school, homework, money, a car, or your curfew may be hard to reach.

When you're in the middle of a shouting match, it might seem impossible to go for win-win. Using the following strategies can help everyone cool down and get what they want.

## SET A TIME AND PLACE TO MEET

Pin down the time and place to talk about a problem. Pick a setting that promotes solutions. If you want to settle a long-standing argument, choose "neutral territory." If you often end up shouting, choose a public place where you have to be quiet or leave, such as a library.

## START WITH SOMETHING EASY

Work on one problem at a time. If the disagreement involves a continuing issue, such as your curfew, it may help to make other, easier agreements first. You may promise to put your clean laundry away or to be home from school at a specific time to watch your younger brother.

## Keep Your Word

Keeping agreements will help build others' trust in you. This sets up a pattern for success. As you build mutual trust, especially with adults, you can move toward taking charge of your life.

When you make and keep agreements, you build a reputation with others—and with yourself. When others know they can count on you to do what you commit to, they may be willing to give you more freedom.

## Brainstorm

Early in the discussion, brainstorm to discover a creative solution. Brainstorming isn't negotiating. Solutions will come up that you won't agree with. That's fine. All ideas that might lead to a solution are useful, even if they seem silly or strange.

## Accept Conflict

Conflict is normal. When people get together, whether it's a family of two or a planet of 5 billion, there will be disagreement.

Be aware that a problem may get worse before it gets better. Once people are willing to work for an agreement and to say what they really think, they might discover that the conflict runs deeper than they assumed.

## Remember the Benefits

When going for the win option seems too hard, take a break. Think about the advantages of resolving the conflict. Imagine how it would feel to be free of the problem. This can give you the energy to keep striving for a win-win solution.

## Slow Down the Pace

In heated discussions people often interrupt each other. You can break that cycle with a simple action. Before replying to someone, wait a few seconds. Then ask, "Is there anything more that you want to say?" This will release tension and calm tempers.

## Get to the Point

Point out exactly what a person *does* or *says* that you don't like. Be specific about how you see the problem and about the solution you want.

## RETURN TO THE PRESENT

Keep the discussion in the present. Avoid dredging up conflicts from the past. Always return to the problem that's on the table right now.

## USE TIME AS AN ALLY

Sometimes conflicts resolve themselves when we wait. If you can't reach a solution that benefits both parties, put off making a final decision for now. Come back to the problem later.

## ALLOW FOR DIFFERENT STYLES

Remember that other people may handle conflict differently than you do. To uncover these differences, ask questions such as "Do you want to talk about this right now?" or "How do you think we can solve this problem?"

## FIND COMMON GROUND

As you begin a discussion, take a minute to find common ground. Remind everyone present about the issues on which you already agree. This sets the stage for a win-win agreement.

## DEFINE THE OUTCOME

Be clear about what you want to happen. Define exactly how you and the other person will know when the outcome has been achieved. For example, you and your mother might have different ideas about what it means to keep your room clean. Talk it over and see if you both can agree on what a clean room looks like.

## SET TIME FRAMES

Set time limits on your agreements. If an agreement works, you can renew it. If an agreement doesn't work, consider revising it and trying that for another week or two. Even agreements that are working may benefit from a few changes.

## CHOOSE WHAT HAPPENS NEXT

Decide in advance what will happen if either of you breaks the agreement. Say that you and your brother agree to stop bugging each other. You might add another item to the agreement: "If I forget and start bothering you, you have the right to walk away."

## WRITE DOWN THE AGREEMENT

Writing helps clarify what your agreement really is, and it helps people remember the terms of the agreement. Consider asking everyone to sign the agreement.

Asking teachers or parents to sign an agreement might seem impolite. If so, make notes about your conversation. They might be willing to read your notes just to check that you both understand.

## MAKE COMMITMENTS

Agreements are most likely to work when everyone promises. Ask each person for a commitment to live by the agreement. If one of you won't commit, keep working for an agreement that *does* win everyone's commitment.

Agreements include possibilities, plans, and promises. Listen for the difference between these levels of commitment:

*Possibility:* "This agreement might work. I'll give it a try."

*Plan:* "I plan to keep this agreement"

*Promise:* "I will keep this agreement. You can count on it."

WORKBOOK PRACTICE 6-3

# Go For The Big Picture

WHEN AGREEMENTS are hard to reach, take a minute to go for the big picture. Imagine that your conflict with the other person is a scene in a movie and that you're in the audience watching the movie for the first time.

The purpose for this mental exercise is to help you view the conflict as a neutral, outside observer would. Doing this gives you a broader perspective, and a broader perspective can loosen up your thinking and spark new solutions.

Suppose you are out with your friend. You want to eat pizza and your friend wants sub sandwiches. The real issue here may not be the food but who gets to choose the restaurant. Instead of arguing, try to see the big picture. Invite your friend to join in:

"It seems to me that we're really arguing about who decides what we do. Let's talk about that, OK?"

Another example: Your mother is mad because you came home late. She threatens to ground you. Your first impulse is to argue or explode with anger. That's a straight path to lose-lose.

Instead, go for the big picture. Observe what's going on without labeling anyone as good or bad. Imagine what everyone in the scene is thinking and feeling.

Now see that your mother worries about your safety. When you don't come home, she senses danger. You see yourself wanting a later curfew. You say:

"Mom, I'm sorry that you were so worried about me. I know you were afraid that something must have happened to me. Tomorrow could we talk about changing my curfew? I want to be able to stay out later, and I don't want you to be scared."

This technique is like using a zoom lens. When you zoom in close to the situation, you see only details: tears, scowls, the knot in your stomach, the desire to shout. Zoom out for a wide-angle view, and the whole scene changes. You see things you didn't notice before. You can bet-

ter understand what each person wants. You realize that you're all in this together and that your chances of reaching agreement are much greater.

Going for the big picture can work even when the conflict is within yourself. Suppose you made a New Year's resolution to finish your homework and you still aren't doing it. Instead of getting down on yourself, take a quick zoom out. In your mind see everything that happens when you don't complete your homework. Look for something in this scene that you can change, something that would allow you to finish your homework. Go for a bigger picture and dissolve the barriers to your goal.

# Communicate With Adults

**W**HEN YOU PRACTICE self-management, mistakes happen. For example, while learning to manage a curfew, you could stay up too late and not get enough sleep. You might feel terrible the next day or even get sick. Often the consequences of mistakes are not serious. Sometimes they are. Anyone who falls asleep while driving can die or kill someone else.

## ASK FOR A CHANCE TO MAKE CHOICES

If there is a task that you want to handle yourself, ask for permission to take it over. Decide with the adult or adults what the consequences of failure will be. If they aren't willing to grant the permission you want right now, ask what you *can* do to show that you're ready for the responsibility.

Suppose your mother tells you to study every evening from 7:00 to 9:00 p.m. Keeping up with your homework is OK with you, and that time is as good as any. Even so, you'd prefer to be responsible for your homework without being ordered to do it. Some teens find this to be so irritating that they refuse to do the work or they do only the minimum needed to get by.

Refusing to work is a poor way to show adults that control doesn't work; it usually sets up a vicious circle. The parent thinks more control is needed. The teen refuses to work harder. So the parent imposes more restrictions and punishments. The teenager resists even more.

Another option is to ask for a chance to make choices. You could use an approach like this:

"If I follow your rules for a week, can I set my own homework hours the following week?"

## RE-SHOOT THAT SCENE

Being with the adults in your life gives you practice in different ways of communicating. In your mind create a video in which the following conversation takes place.

**Parent:** I'm upset that you came home so late last night. I didn't get much sleep. I was afraid you were getting into trouble or were in an accident or something.

**Teenager:** Why do you worry so much? I'm fine. I don't need you to tell me what to do!

Now rewind the tape and rewrite the scene:

**Parent:** I'm upset that you came home so late last night. I didn't get much sleep. I was afraid you were getting into trouble or were in an accident or something.

**Teenager:** Gee, I'm sorry you're tired and upset because I got home late last night.

Which scene is more likely to end with a win-win agreement? During your teen years, you get to do this kind of rewinding and rewriting in real life. At times you might feel that parents, teachers, and other adults in your life are from another country—or another planet. Even when you try to listen, it still seems as if you're speaking different languages.

## KEEP WORKING AT IT

Using methods from this chapter to listen and speak can make a big difference. Reaching agreements with adults, however, can be hard even with the best communication techniques. Here are some more ideas:

Before tackling a tough problem, do something that you all enjoy. Have some fun together.

Ask adults for their opinions about another key issue. This lets them know that you value their ideas.

Choose your battles. Be willing to give in sometimes and do what adults ask, especially on minor issues.

Establish agreements about important issues in advance, such as curfew, dating, driving, and use of the telephone.

Admit errors and mistakes. If you're wrong, apologize.

Move from getting to giving. Instead of asking, "What's in this for me?" ask, "How can I help in this situation?"

Express appreciation. Thank the adults for something they've done recently. You can do this even when you don't feel thankful at the moment.

Perform a "secret service"—a small, considerate act for an important adult in your life. Don't seek credit or praise for this service. If you get confused, remember the suggestion to "practice random acts of kindness, senseless acts of beauty." Then enjoy the results.

WORKBOOK
PRACTICE 6-6

WORKBOOK
JOURNAL 6-7

# Don't Try This At Home

**S**OME ADULTS will not appreciate your practicing some of the suggestions in this chapter. To them, listening actively or speaking effectively is the same as talking back and being disrespectful. If this happens, try some other options:

Put your request in writing.

Go to members of your extended family for support.

Enlist outside help. Find a person from the community whom your parents respect and ask them to speak on your behalf.

Ask older brothers or sisters how they managed.

Demonstrate that you are trust-worthy and responsible.

Keep the big picture. You won't live with your parents forever.

# Call A Family Meeting

REGULAR MEETINGS of people who live together help keep relationships working. Family meetings provide each person with opportunities, to agree about chores, to resolve arguments, to express feelings and complaints, to encourage other family members, and to help plan family activities.

Family meetings are times for parents to tell teens how they would like for them to behave. They are also times for children to tell parents how they want to be treated. These meetings offer a place for people to talk about the things that are most difficult or troublesome.

Meeting once a week is ideal. Some families begin meetings with each person talking about the week, giving compliments, doing something fun, or with a prayer. Other families save those activities for the end of the meeting, after problems have been aired.

Consider rotating leadership and notetaking responsibilities for the meeting. You can post a record of agreements and promises in a prominent place.

At the first meeting, ask each person what ground rules will help establish an atmosphere of cooperation, respect, and problem solving. When everyone has agreed on the meeting rules, post them and review them frequently.

Everyone has the right to say what is on his mind without being interrupted or criticized. The needs, wants, feelings, and responsibilities of each family member deserve fair consideration. Keep in mind that adults control the house and most of the money. They are also legally responsible for their children. Resisting this reality is counterproductive.

Use a weekly meeting to tell each other what you want and how you feel. When there are specific issues to be resolved, first agree on how to talk about the issue. Then work on a solution that everyone is willing to try.

It's OK to start discussing a problem and then let it rest. A workable solution may surface after everyone has had time to think. Sometimes, just talking about a problem handles it. Don't expect to fix every problem in one meeting. Family meetings that accomplish much and that respect those involved take practice.

WORKBOOK
KEY WORDS

WORKBOOK
PRACTICE 6-8

WORKBOOK
PROGRESS CHECK

WORKBOOK
OUTLINE

# Chapter 7 Objectives

After mastering this chapter you will be able to:

- BUILD A SUPPORT NETWORK

- FIND AND USE A TUTOR

- USE MISTAKES AS FEEDBACK

# CHAPTER MAKE IT A TEAM EFFORT

# Build Your Team

THERE IS NO NEED to go it alone. Successful people usually have a network of people who offer guidance and support along the way. You can begin building such a team for yourself right now. Here are some ideas to help you do this.

## BE SOMEONE YOU'D LIKE TO MEET

You spend most of your time with one person—yourself. Become one of your own favorite people. When you're comfortable with yourself, others are more easily drawn to you.

## BE A FRIEND

To gain a friend, be a friend. If you want support, give it first to others. Look for opportunities to encourage and support all of the people in your life, and the same will come back to you.

## CHOOSE YOUR FRIENDS AND STICK TO YOUR VALUES

Think about your values. What do you consider most important in life? Who do you want to be? What do you want to do and have over the next few years? Put your thoughts in writing to help you gain clarity. Choose friends who will support you in getting what you want. Avoid people who set conditions on friendship ("I'll be your friend if...") or who ask you to do things that violate your values.

## STAY IN CHARGE

Going along with the crowd is easy. You let other people do the thinking, and you just choose what they choose. Unfortunately, the crowd will probably go somewhere that you don't want to be.

Ask yourself, "Am I choosing here, or are my friends?" The answer can make a big difference in your choices about music, clothes, career, sex, smoking, alcohol and other drugs, and a host of other issues. Self-confidence comes with deciding for yourself. As you practice choosing for yourself, you'll make friends who notice and respect this quality in you.

## LET THE REAL YOU SHOW THROUGH

Make a habit of saying what you really think and feel. Chances are that others are thinking and feeling the same things. If you tell people only what you think they want to hear, you end up disguising yourself.

## GET SOME STUDY BUDDIES

"If you want to learn a subject, teach it to someone else" is good advice. Your fellow students are also your fellow teachers. Organize a small group of friends, meet regularly, and teach each other the content of your classes. It's a great way to build your social network and to succeed in school at the same time.

## FIND MENTORS

A **mentor** is a person who believes in your potential and is willing to help you achieve it. Look for someone you know and respect. Ask her about her life. Observe the traits you admire and practice them. You can have several mentors, different ones for different skills.

WORKBOOK
JOURNAL 7-1

# Recruit Your Parents

YOUR EDUCATION is your job. At the same time, the adults you live with (parent or parents, step-parents, foster parents, legal guardians, relatives, or other adults responsible for you) have a major role to play. Here are some ideas about getting the **support** you need with the least amount of hassle.

## ASK FOR HELP

When you find yourself in a situation that you don't know how to handle or that you aren't handling as well as you'd like, you might think, "I could use some help with this, but if I ask my mom or stepdad for help, they'll just take over and start telling me what to do."

Lots of families get caught in this conflict. Following is an example of asking for help without sacrificing independence.

"Mom, I could use some ideas about something. I want to figure out how to handle it myself after I hear your thoughts."

Parents naturally want to help their children become responsible adults. You naturally want **independence**. Being independent calls for three things from both you and your parents: confidence in your ability, willingness to let go, and practice.

Having a supportive relationship with the adults in your family takes practice. Problems may arise when your level of confidence in your own abilities is different from your parents.

You might be sure that you can handle driving right now, and your parents are sure you need to wait. Or your parents may believe that you can travel alone across the state to your cousin's house, but you don't think it's a good idea.

## GET 200 PERCENT

You might think of dividing responsibility with your parents. Say, 50 percent for you and 50 percent for your parent, for a total of 100 percent. But life is more than simple arithmetic. Both you and your parent can assume 100 percent responsibility.

In other words, you are 100 percent responsible for your role, and your parent or parents are 100 percent responsible for their roles in your education. That adds up to 200 percent responsible.

All of your teachers can be 100 percent responsible too. Even though it sounds strange, it works. For example, in many jobs the manager is 100 percent responsible for getting the work done. Supervisors are 100 percent responsible for their departments. Finally, each employee is 100 percent responsible for his assigned tasks.

In the family, parents and teens are each totally responsible for different tasks, and those tasks change over time. Your parents' confidence in you will increase when you agree on the tasks, promise to complete them fully, and follow through.

## LET GO

Letting go is a two-way street. Your parents' confidence in you is based on their perception of how you handle things like doing chores and homework, being on time, following through on commitments, spending money.

When you've been acting very grown up, you may wonder why your parents don't treat you as an adult. They are likely to treat you as the person they see most often, not the older person you occasionally show up to be like. You want them to let go of their old pictures of who you are.

You also need to let go of being a child. Your parents won't think of you as a young adult if they frequently have to step in and handle your responsibilities. These responsibilities might include taking care of younger children in your family, staying within the budget, doing yard work, shopping for groceries, doing laundry, or arranging for transportation.

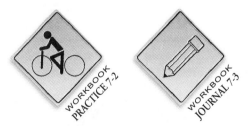

# Hire a Tutor

TUTORS ARE PRIVATE instructors. A tutor can be almost anyone—a friend, a classmate, a teacher, a parent, some other adult, or another student who excels in the subject.

Consider a tutor if you are having trouble in a course or if you want to master something you need before taking a new course.

Tutoring is not just another hour in school with the tutor substituting for your teacher. Instead, a tutor is your personal coach, and your time together is like a workout. As your coach, a tutor explains, answers questions, and demonstrates while you practice to mastery.

A tutor's job is to assist you. When working with a tutor:

Ask questions.

Ask for explanations to be repeated, restated, or stopped.

Change the subject if your thoughts take a different path from the tutor's.

Decide when you have seen enough and are ready to practice.

Ask for and get as much help as you want during practice.

Decide when you have practiced enough and are ready to be tested.

## ASK QUESTIONS AND MAKE REQUESTS

When you work with a tutor, you can ask more questions and make more requests than you can in class. Here are some examples:

What is the big picture?
What am I supposed to learn to do?
Describe that in terms I understand.
What is the purpose of doing it?
How long does it take most people
    to learn it?
How will I be tested?
What should I already know?
Tell me how to do it.
Please stop talking.
Tell me about this.
Tell me again.
Tell me in a different way.

Tell me in more detail.
Tell me in less detail.
Explain what this is.
Define that word.
How do you know what to do?
How do you know when to do it?
How do you know when to stop?
Show me how to do that.
Show me again.
Show me more slowly.
Tell me what you're doing as you do it.
Show me a simpler situation.
Show me a more complex situation.
Let me try.
Is it safe to do this?
How long would it take you
    to do this?
How long should it take me
    to do this?
Watch me.
Remind me how to start.
Remind me what to do next.
Is this the next step?
Is this right?
Should I keep trying?
Have I missed a step?
Have I done something wrong?
How am I doing?
Which parts did I do well?
What could I have done better?
Do I need more practice?
What else you should tell me now?
Have I mastered this?
What else would I have to do to
    demonstrate mastery?

## YOU'RE IN CHARGE

Clarify—up front—the kind of relationship you want with your tutor. Ask the tutor to let you direct your time together and to be patient. Tell her that you will be practicing during the tutoring session, or that you will be doing your homework while she watches. Request that she coach you as you practice.

Suppose you are having trouble with a math problem and you ask your tutor to show you how to solve it. She may say, "If I do that, you won't learn for yourself." To that, you respond, "Yes, I will. I'm going to practice on this type of problem until I achieve mastery. If you'd rather, you can show me how to solve a similar problem, then I'll do this one on my own."

To help explain the type of relationship you want, ask your tutor to read this article. You can follow these suggestions even if your parent is doing the tutoring. Once a tutor understands your mastery learning process, you will probably get the kind of help you can best use.

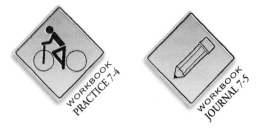

WORKBOOK PRACTICE 7-4

WORKBOOK JOURNAL 7-5

# Think of Teachers as Allies

TEACHERS ARE GUIDES who can help you plan, prepare to practice, do the practice, and get feedback. Some will be excellent guides, and some won't. The point is this: You can do what it takes to gain mastery, regardless of how much you like your teachers or how well they perform.

Teachers show students how to practice. For example, they demonstrate solving algebra problems or analyzing novels. They give assignments and check the work to see that the student is progressing.

Teachers also manage class discussions. They provide guidance and encouragement, complimenting good work, correcting mistakes, and assisting students.

Some teachers do these things better than others. With some you may feel encouraged and motivated. Around other teachers, you might feel bored or incompetent. Either way, all teachers are potentially helpful to you as you learn. You can turn teachers into allies by keeping one thing in mind: School is not about giving teachers grades for popularity; school is about your learning.

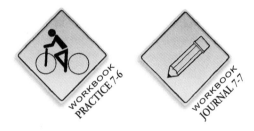

WORKBOOK PRACTICE 7-6

WORKBOOK JOURNAL 7-7

# Love Those Mistak'<sub>e</sub>s

MASTERS OF MOST crafts praise the value of taking intelligent risks and making mistakes. A Yiddish proverb says, "He who lies on the ground cannot fall." Mistakes are great teachers. As we practice to mastery, mistakes are expected and are often unavoidable. Don't let them throw you into a tailspin.

Risking mistakes and failures can be scary and embarrassing. Ask the skater who sprawls on the ice during a performance or the novelist whose best work is rejected by a publisher. Ask the artist who stages a one-person show, and the only ones who show up are his mother and his dog. When you pursue your dreams, mistakes and failures are part of the chase.

This is not to say that you should make mistakes on purpose. Taking risks is not the same as being sloppy or careless. And being willing to look foolish is not the same as acting like a fool. The message here is to set out to do your best and to take a new view of the mistakes as they happen.

Replace the word failure with feedback. If you fail a test, that's just feedback telling you to examine how you are preparing for tests. If you can't read your own notes, that's feedback too. It says, "Write more clearly when you take notes."

Mistakes happen. They can be your friends, committed to your success in life. Think of your mistakes as feedback to help you change direction and get back on track.

WORKBOOK PRACTICE 7-8

# Savor Success

A S YOU BEGIN to experience the learning curve, you may be frustrated with your slow initial progress. When you focus only on the things you have left to do, it's easy to forget about what you have already done. To help keep things in perspective, savor your success along the way toward your goals.

That's the idea behind the Success Log suggested in Chapter 1. Notice anything and everything you've done well. Take pride in your accomplishments, even the small ones. Honestly listing your achievements and pausing to enjoy them can boost your energy level and increase your interest in moving ahead.

Also, review your goals and action plans from time to time. If everything seems to be working, you can stay with the same plan. But not getting the results you want is a wake-up call that says it's time to change plans.

Feedback from yourself is one of the most powerful ways to stay on track. Straying off course is fine if you notice that it is happening and you take corrective action. Just remember to congratulate yourself for the miles you cover as you zero in on your goals.

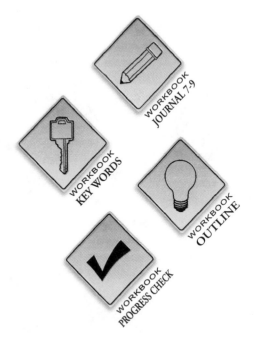

# Chapter 8 Objectives

After mastering this chapter you will be able to:

- EVALUATE FACTORS THAT INFLUENCE HOW YOU FEEL ABOUT YOURSELF

- IMPROVE YOUR SELF-CONFIDENCE

- MANAGE YOUR RESPONSE TO DIFFICULT EMOTIONS

# CHAPTER **RESPECT YOURSELF**

8

# Take a Look in the Mirror

**T**HIS BOOK OFFERS chances for you to set goals, plan actions, and see how you're doing. Within each is an opportunity to take a simple, powerful action: Hold up a mirror to yourself. Many people would rather do just about anything than take stock of themselves. That's easy to understand. What we find is not always what we want to see.

If we avoid **self-examination** we miss the chance to be happier, more productive, and more successful. Getting to that place calls for a courageous act—telling the truth about what's working in our lives and what is not.

Like most of the techniques suggested in *Learning Power,* looking deeply into the mirror becomes easier and more effective with practice. You learn not to judge or label yourself as bad or stupid. In fact, as you develop the skill of honest self-assessment, your self-esteem will grow.

Self-awareness is a quality unique to the human being. If you want your life to work, then self-awareness is your constant ally. Look in the mirror often, and tell the truth about what you see. When you see something you don't like, you can decide to do something about it. Your awareness will help focus your energy for personal change.

WORKBOOK
JOURNAL 8-1

# Revisit the Change Process

**A**FTER COMPLETING the "Getting Personal" survey in your workbook, you may have a list of things to improve. You can chip away at your list using the **Change Process**. If you're unclear about any of the steps, review "Adopt a Process for Change" in Chapter 1. Here are the steps:

1. Be Aware
2. Take responsibility
3. Forgive
4. Change
5. Practice
6. Get feedback

Remember, the Change Process is a way to improve or eliminate any negative situation in your life. The idea is simple. To get a different response from the world around you, change what you do.

The fourth step in the Change Process is worth a few more words. This step calls for action—doing something new or different from what you have been doing.

Sometimes the needed change is obvious. Say, for example, you want to exercise more, so you decide to jog every morning before breakfast. That's a sensible way to get exercise. And if it doesn't work, you can choose something that does. If you don't know what to change or if the change you've tried hasn't worked, you still have many options:

Get suggestions from a book or audiotape. Maybe a friend, librarian, or clerk at the video rental store can recommend a book or tape that's on track for you.

Get help from an expert. Your school, church, club, or family can help you find one.

Get help from your friends or family. Ask these people to brainstorm with you. Create a lot of possibilities without judging any of them. Then see if any of the possibilities actually make sense.

Be your own adviser. Think about what you would say to someone who came to you with the same problem. Then consider applying your own suggestions.

WORKBOOK PRACTICE 8-2

# Befriend Your Body

**Y**OUR BODY IS YOURS to care for. It enables you to do what you want. People have all kinds of ideas about what you should put in it, put on it, and do with it. You get to choose. Take care of yourself for *yourself,* not because someone else says you should.

## IMAGE ADVERTISING

We all have powerful messages coming at us about how our bodies are supposed to look. Huge businesses depend on our thinking there is something wrong with how we look, how we are built, and even how we smell.

When you believe that you need to change something to be attractive or cool, you are motivated to buy something. Advertisers will never tell you, "You are just fine. You don't need anything to be OK." They spend big money to convince you that just the opposite is true.

We are all familiar with "the look"— the totally cool, gorgeous young men and women we see on the covers of magazines, on the TV soap operas and on product packages. That image is not actually achievable! If it were, we would achieve it and we would stop spending money on the next false promise.

## DESPERATE MEASURES

No two bodies are alike. Real people don't look much like the pictures of people you see in movies or magazines. The teenage desire to look like the stars can be so strong that it damages self-esteem, takes all available money, and sometimes leads to serious health problems.

Desperate to look different, some people take extreme measures; using steroids to help build muscle; having plastic surgery to change facial features; or piercing, scarring, and tattooing skin. These behaviors come from the belief that who we are isn't good enough and that if we do these things we will be.

In our society the pressure to be thin is intense. Most bodies wouldn't be healthy if they were as thin as our cultural ideal.

This ideal is crippling to many young people. They can no longer see their bodies for what they are. In their eyes they look fat, so they diet to the point of avoiding food almost completely. This condition, called anorexia nervosa, affects thousands of people, including models, movie stars, athletes, and ordinary people.

Bulemia is another illness that affects thousands of teenagers. A bulemic person binges (eats enormous quantities of food) and then purges (makes herself vomit). These eating disorders can cause permanent physical damage or death.

## BEAUTY IS IN THE EYE OF THE BEHOLDER

Keep in mind that standards of beauty change. In the sixteenth century, the most beautiful women were quite large ("fat" by today's standards). In some cultures the rulers are extremely fat, a symbol of their importance, their wealth, and of the fact that they do no physical work. Nineteenth century women obtained seventeen-inch waists by cinching themselves into whalebone corsets.

People of all shapes and sizes create loving relationships, fulfilling careers, and happy lives. You are unique. Your "flaws," along with your best features, make you that way. A big part of growing up is learning to accept, appreciate, and care for the body you were born with.

## ENJOY A HEALTHY BODY

Poor health is a hassle. People who are tired, stressed out, or sick may feel frustrated, unhappy, and that their lives are out of control. You may want to make some improvements in your health.

First, if you need it, get help from a doctor, dentist, or other health professional. Make an appointment now.

Second, take care of yourself. Eat well, exercise, and drink lots of water.

Third, get adequate sleep. If you have trouble getting up in the morning, that's a pretty good indication that you need more sleep. If so, experiment by going to bed thirty to sixty minutes earlier each night for a week. See for yourself if the benefits are worth the time it takes.

## HEALTH AND THE CHANGE PROCESS

People who succeed at caring for their bodies have a knack for succeeding in general. The same skills that help you excel at doing homework can help you master caring for your body. Here's how the Change Process (see pages 19-20, 125) can help change health habits—some of the toughest habits to break.

Roberto, for example, wants to start exercising regularly. The six steps of the Change Process can help him succeed.

### STEP 1: AWARENESS

Roberto begins by admitting the truth: He hardly ever exercises.

### STEP 2: RESPONSIBILITY

He could easily say, "I'm just not cut out for exercise; I'm not the athletic type." Instead, he chooses to say, "I'm going to work out at least three times each week."

### STEP 3: FORGIVENESS

Roberto remembers that he has tried to work out regularly before. He tells the truth about this, too, and chooses to try again.

### STEP 4: CHANGE

He concludes that exercising didn't work before because he put it off until late at night. Roberto's new plan is to work out right after school on Tuesdays, Thursdays, and Fridays.

### STEP 5: PRACTICE

On Tuesday everything proceeds according to plan. Roberto jogs home from school instead of taking the bus. He does pushups, sit-ups, and chin-ups. It feels great. He just knows this exercise plan is going to work.

On Thursday Roberto hangs out with friends after school a little longer than usual. He's late for his exercise appointment, but he still manages to jog before dinner.

Friday Roberto forgets his exercise program and goes to the mall with his girlfriend after school. Suddenly his prospects for "abs of steel" aren't looking so bright.

### STEP 6: FEEDBACK

This is the point where Roberto could trash his exercise plan. Instead, he returns to Step 3 and revises his plan. He writes his exercise schedule on a calendar and will highlight each day that he exercises. He promises to reward himself with a new compact disk after working out regularly for one month.

This time Roberto's plan works. Soon he's getting feedback from his calendar, his stronger body, and his growing CD collection.

WORKBOOK JOURNAL 8-3    WORKBOOK PRACTICE 8-4

# Be Truthful

PEOPLE TELL LIES in order to hide something they did or something they are thinking about doing. Or they may lie to prevent embarrassment or other painful feelings. Or they try to avoid having to take responsibility. People often lie to cover up previous lies. Lying can become a very destructive habit.

The saying "What goes around comes around" is a way of describing how the world works. When people lie, they invite certain consequences into their lives:

## LIARS ISOLATE THEMSELVES

When we lie, we cut others off from the truth about ourselves, and we deny them the chance to really know us. That promotes loneliness. People don't want to hang around with someone they can't trust.

## LYING COMPLICATES LIFE

The more someone lies, the harder he have to work to keep all the stories straight. Lying becomes a trap, and sooner or later things begin to unravel. Self-confidence suffers.

## LYING DENIES SELF-KNOWLEDGE

Being untruthful has a negative effect on a person's sense of self. And the more one lies, the more difficult it is to know what the truth really is. When people believe their own lies, they become confused by the reactions of others. They can't understand why people are leaving them, avoiding them, or discriminating against them.

At times it can be very hard to tell the truth. It takes courage to consistently speak and act honestly. But, over the long term, being truthful will build friendship, confidence, and self-esteem. It is a great value to practice.

WORKBOOK PRACTICE 8-5

# Gain Self-Confidence

SELF-CONFIDENCE affects what you do every day. People with high self-confidence are willing to make new friends, take on challenging projects, and set goals for the future. Those who lack confidence do such things less often—sometimes not at all. Self-confidence isn't something you are born with. It is developed over time.

## GIVE YOUR WORD

You can detect self-confidence in the things people say:

"I always mess up on math tests."
"I'll never be better at writing than I am right now."
"I can't get the job I really want."

When people say such things, their actions usually follow suit. These statements reveal the way they think, and this way of thinking rules out any new options for the future.

Words can lead the way into new thinking and acting. Watch out for words like *always*, *never*, and *can't*. In their place, say *sometimes*, *can*, or *could*:

"I sometimes mess up on math tests."
"I could be better at writing than I am now."
"I can get the job I really want."

## ACT ON YOUR WORD

Ask yourself, "If I really believed these things, what would I *do*?" If you want to get better at writing, perhaps you could ask an English teacher for extra help, or practice writing every day.

The next step is to follow through by doing those things, even if you don't think they'll work. While you're at it, practice speaking in a way that helps you change.

It's hard to directly change the way you feel about yourself. Even so, you can almost always change what you say and then what you *do*. As you practice speaking and acting in new ways, you will notice the difference in your level of self-confidence —and your life.

## FOCUS ON SKILLS

Self-confidence and skills are linked. As people gain skills, they generally gain self-confidence too.

Most of this book is about helping you gain self-confidence. By reading *Learning Power* and using *The Learning Power Workbook*, you can gain skills that will make a big difference in your life. Some of these are study skills. Others are skills at getting along with people—listening, speaking, reaching agreements. Also important are skills at managing yourself, such as setting goals and making decisions.

## TAKE RESPONSIBILITY

A big part of growing up is learning to separate what you can change from what you cannot. For instance, you cannot change your genes. Genes determine how tall you are, whether you're male or female, and a host of other things about you. You can change how you respond to these facts. If you're short, you can still play basketball. If you're female, you can be a smart, assertive, analytical, outspoken leader in any career field.

You control the decisions you make, and you can always change your mind. The student who feels like fainting before giving a speech can decide never to speak in front of a class again. Or he can decide to speak in class every chance he gets, knowing that practice will help him gain skills and self-confidence.

When we control our decisions and change what we can, we are taking responsibility. Gaining self-confidence is one of the rewards.

## EXPRESS APPRECIATION

Your self-confidence can grow when others appreciate your developing skills. Almost everyone enjoys hearing "You did a great job" or "I can't wait to read your next paper."

Appreciation is most meaningful when it comes naturally. You can't force others to express sincere appreciation. However, you can set an example by expressing your thanks for what they say and do. This will likely result in more positive feedback coming your way.

WORKBOOK PRACTICE 8-6    WORKBOOK JOURNAL 8-7

# Win Positive Respect

There are two different kinds of respect. By acting tough, some people incite others' fear. They enjoy fearful respect only for as long as it takes people to get away from them. Positive regard from students, your parents, and your teachers requires other approaches.

## Do Unto Others

It's easy to focus on how other people disappoint you—what they do or fail to do, what they say or forget to say. Instead of resenting them, set an example. If you want to be treated with courtesy, be courteous. If you want others to listen when you speak, listen when *they* speak. Your kindness will find its way back to you.

## Go for Win-Win

Ask for what you want while making room for what others want. See Chapter 6 for ideas.

## Deliver on Your Word

First, *give* your word by making promises, reaching agreements, and stating your plans. Then *keep* your word by following through. When others know that they can count on you, they will respect you, and you'll know that you can count on yourself.

# Stop Sexual Harassment

*Girl:* Thanks for taking me to the movie. It was great.

*Boy:* No problem. You mean a lot to me.

*Girl:* I like you a lot too.

*Boy:* Cool. (He tries to kiss her.)

*Girl:* That's nice, but . . . I'd like to go home.

*Boy:* Forget home. You're with me now. (Holds her tighter and tries to kiss her again.)

*Girl:* Ouch! Let go. I really need to go home.

*Boy:* Not so fast. I spent a lot of money on you tonight. You owe me. The least you can do is kiss me.

This is a clear example of sexual harassment. In a 1993 study of American public schools, two-thirds of the girls said they'd been sexually harassed at school. Half of the boys also reported being sexually harassed. This harassment took many forms, from bra-snapping and teasing to grabbing and forced kissing.

Television may lead us to believe that sexual harassment is funny. In one comedy, a teenage character strolls up to a woman and asks, "Would you like to hear my recipe for a love cocktail?" On another show, a policewoman shouts at a man, "Hey, Sugar Buns! Move it along." It's no wonder that sexual harassment happens in the hallways, cafeterias, and locker rooms of our schools.

Students say that when they experience sexual harassment, it is hard to concentrate on homework or talk in class. Some students in the 1993 survey said that sexual harassment made them wonder if they could ever finish high school.

People might try to tell you that sexual harassment is something everyone does, that it is just part of going to school. Don't believe it. You have the right to decide when you want to talk about sex and how you want to be touched. There are several things you can do to protect that right.

## Set Limits

Decide what kind of comments and touching mean sexual harassment to you.

## Speak Up

The first time someone goes beyond your limits, tell them loud and clear. You can even put your comments in writing: "Julie, please quit trying to hug me in front of all your friends in the lunchroom. It really bothers me."

## Report It

If someone keeps bothering you after you have clearly told them to stop, report it to a teacher or administrator.

## Enforce Rules

Find out if your school has a policy on sexual harassment. It should define exactly what sexual harassment is and provide tough penalties, including fines and suspension. If not, contact the parent-teacher group and ask them to develop one.

## Don't Join In

When you see sexual harassment happening, refuse to be part of it. Stand with the person being harassed and look at the person who is doing it. Speak your objection.

## Refuse to Make Excuses

Comments like "Boys will be boys" or "She always acts like that in front of her friends" don't cut it. You should never have to put up with sexual harassment.

WORKBOOK PRACTICE 8-8

# Manage TOUGH Emotions

**I**MAGINE A WORLD where people feel no emotions. They attend weddings, funerals, graduations, and parties without feeling a thing. That world would be as exciting as a bowl of day-old oatmeal.

We can be thankful that we don't inhabit such a world. Feelings are the spice of life. And sometimes life gets a little *too* spicy. Emotions can be so strong and unpleasant that we feel a loss of control.

It's normal to feel sad, angry, or afraid at times. But when strong negative feelings stick around for months or years, it is hard to carry out the tasks of daily life. We might need help from a professional counselor or psychologist. You can handle difficult feelings before they become a serious problem by following these suggestions.

## ACCEPT YOUR FEELINGS

Emotions are like weather. They are changeable and unpredictable. Moods come and go, often for no apparent reason. If you're having a feeling you don't like, just wait. It will likely pass. A new feeling will take its place, even if you do nothing.

Feelings are tough to control. Few of us can summon up emotional feelings on command. Imagine that a friend walks up to you and says, "You have two more minutes to feel sad. Then I want you to feel happy. Start now, and I'll time you." Most of us would have a hard time complying.

You don't have to apologize for your feelings. They are not good or bad, moral or immoral. They are just feelings. Instead of trying to fix the feelings, you can simply accept them.

Our feelings are beyond our direct control. However, we can *influence* them indirectly by using the next three strategies.

## TALK TO YOURSELF IN A NEW WAY

People who often feel sad, angry, or afraid usually talk in ways that keep them trapped:

"I always get sick during
  finals week."
"She has no right to act that way."
"Things just can't turn out
  like this."
"I don't want to do this, but I
  have to."
"You can forget about trying
  to change me."

There are some irrational beliefs underlying the previous statements:

"One time I got really sick during
  finals week, so I know I'll always
  get sick during finals week."
"People should always act the
  way I want them to."
"Events should always turn out
  as I expect."
"What choice do I have? I have
  to do what others say."
"I can't change."

Think about these beliefs. Most of them are self-defeating. Notice that they contain words such as *always*, *can't*, and *have to*. Listen for these kinds of statements in your own speaking. Write out the underlying beliefs and think about them. Do these beliefs serve you? Do they bring you closer to your goals, or do they make you happier?

As a related experiment, change your speaking. Change *can't* to *could*; *have to* to *want to*; *always* to *sometimes*. Then see if your actions fit with your new speaking. The results might surprise you.

## TALK TO SOMEONE ELSE

Emotions can get stronger when we bottle them up or try to force ourselves not to feel them. There's a saying, "What we resist, persists." That is, the more we try to push away an unpleasant feeling, the more it pushes back.

Find a friend who is willing to listen. Sometimes it pays to ask a professional listener, such as a counselor or minister, for help.

## TAKE ACTION

Emotion is motion. If you want to *feel* differently, then *move* differently. Even the simplest actions—walking or jogging, calling a friend, taking a nap—can shift our feelings in profound ways.

It is very powerful to realize that you can have your emotions without your emotions having you. You can feel a whole range of feelings, no matter how unpleasant, without acting on them. You don't have to be a prisoner of your feelings.

Acting on your emotions or not acting on them are choices you can make. Even when you feel lazy, you can still choose to do homework. When you feel like sleeping, you still have the ability to get out of bed. When you are depressed, you can still make your bed, take out the garbage, and bake cookies. You can say "I love you" even when you are mad at someone. You can walk on stage even when you feel stage fright.

WORKBOOK PRACTICE 8-9

WORKBOOK JOURNAL 8-10

# Employ the
# Social Graces

**R**ELATIONSHIPS are built slowly over time and are cemented by hundreds of acts of simple courtesy. Social graces never go out of style.

Contrary to an old slogan, nice people do finish first. Observe the people you admire most. Chances are, they are polite and courteous.

Practicing social etiquette costs little and has big benefits. Everyday courtesy paves the way for resolving bigger conflicts later on. Besides, when you're polite, your friends (and even their parents) are more likely to invite you back!

Humble words and phrases carry profound meaning. Please admits our need for help and the support of others. Thank you acknowledges the skills and resources freely given by others. Yes, sir, No, ma'am, and similar phrases communicate respect.

In addition to these kind words, consider the following ideas.

## RESPOND TO REQUESTS

When we leave questions unanswered or ignore requests, we might send an unwanted message: "I don't consider you or your needs to be important. "Responding to another person's request says, "I value you."

## OTHERS MAY "DO COURTESY" DIFFERENTLY

Be sensitive to the customs of different cultures. What seems courteous to you might seem odd, funny, or even rude to someone from another race or ethnic group. It makes sense to find out the customs of other people in advance. If a situation has turned uncomfortable, ask, "Did I say something to offend you? Do you want me to do something differently?"

## OFFER HELP

Each day presents dozens of opportunities to help others. You can hold open doors, smile, greet people, introduce yourself, and listen with attention. These acts can be fun to do, and they make the world a more pleasant place.

## BE KIND TO ALL

It may be easier to be kind to a special friend than to other people. Experiment with being pleasant, courteous, and helpful to your parents, your brothers and sisters, your teachers, everybody. See what a difference it can make.

WORKBOOK
JOURNAL 8-11

# Defuse Depression

YOU MAY HAVE HEARD someone who's depressed say, "I was so down that I just couldn't do anything." Trying to take action when you're depressed can feel like running through waist-deep mud.

Sometimes we can tie **depression** to a certain event, such as a death. At other times, we don't have a specific reason for feeling sad; it just happens. Emotions that go up and down are part of being human. Short periods of having the blues are normal.

When you feel depressed, see "Manage Tough Emotions" on pages 135-37. Also consider the ideas that follow.

## ALLOW FOR MOOD SWINGS

Feelings are chemistry. During the teen years, your body chemistry undergoes big changes. Endocrine glands release hormones that help you grow and develop into an adult. Along with these new hormones come mood swings. They are normal, and they will pass.

## REMEMBER THE CLICHÉS

Many sayings about sad feelings are overused **clichés**. But they are true and useful. For example, "Into each life some rain must fall" reminds us that everyone suffers. "When life gives you lemons, make lemonade" says that we can choose how to respond to every experience. "Take it easy" reminds us to be gentle with ourselves and that scolding ourselves for feeling depressed is offtrack.

"This too shall pass" tells us that feelings are like waves—they rise, fall, and pass away. Knowing this can be freeing. Painful feelings will fade with time, and feelings of pleasure will wash over us again. Instead of trying to control the waves, we can ride them.

## GET MOVING

Try this experiment the next time you feel low. Stand up straight. Take five deep breaths. Go outside and walk briskly, jog, or run. Smile to yourself or at someone else. Notice what happens to your depressed feelings.

This technique is no substitute for solving problems or handling responsibilities. However, it can help you through emotional rough spots.

## BE THERE FOR OTHERS

When talking to someone else who's depressed, avoid trying to cheer him up. Also, avoid arguing with him or saying, "I know just how you feel." Those tactics can backfire, leading to a response such as "No, you *don't* know how I feel." Just get across the simple message that you care and are willing to help.

This strategy has a side benefit. When you're feeling depressed, focusing your attention on someone else could give you a real lift.

## TALK ABOUT IT

Negative feelings can worsen when they remain inside us. The simple act of sharing your feelings with a sympathetic listener can bring relief.

## WRITE A LETTER TO YOURSELF

Writing about your feelings can heal them, much like talking about them can. Write about your feelings in a journal, and you might gain new insights.

Over time you may see patterns and begin to understand what triggers your depression.

If you are having problems with someone, but you can't talk to them about it, write a letter about how you are feeling. Don't mail the letter when you're finished. Just the act of writing may help release the feelings and lead to healing.

## GIVE A GIFT

Counter depression with an act of gratitude. When you're sad, buy or make a gift for a friend and deliver it in person. Or perform a simple act of service, such as picking up trash in the street or washing the kitchen floor. Simple acts like these can pick up your spirits.

## FACE FEELINGS WHERE YOU ARE

Some people run away from home or school when they're depressed. Many times the old problems still exist in a new place. There is a saying that demonstrates the folly of these escapes: "Wherever you go, there you are."

When we accept our feelings, talk them over with someone, and do something constructive, we are more likely to move through depression. These things may not be easy, but they work.

## FIND ONE GOOD THING

A funny thing happens to our thinking when we feel depressed. We tend to dwell on the negative. A simple shift in attention can change that. When you're sad, look for one thing in your life that you're thankful for—a piece of music, a friend, a pleasant experience, anything. Talk about this one thing for a while or write about it in detail.

## SET A TIME LIMIT

One way to let feelings run their course is to give them full rein for a while. Set a time limit for feeling depressed. Say to yourself, "I'll give myself permission to feel really bad for another twenty-four hours. Then I'm going to get busy and make room for other feelings."

## HOLD A PITY PARTY

Throw a "pity party" for yourself. Watch sad movies. Bring Kleenex. Invite friends to be bummed out with you. (Don't be surprised or disappointed if your depression ends before the party does.)

## PLAN FOR CHANGE

Sometimes depression is a sign that we have problems that need to be handled. You might notice that certain situations trigger your depression. If so, plan how to change them.

## ASK FOR HELP

Depression can be a serious condition, especially when it lasts a while. If you feel depressed for longer periods than usual, get help. Talk to someone your age or to a parent, teacher, clergy, or counselor—anyone you trust. If no one is around, look up the number for a crisis hotline in the phone book and call. It could be the most important call you make.

WORKBOOK PRACTICE 8-12

# Be Alert to **Suicide Talk**

YOU DON'T HAVE to be "crazy" to think about killing yourself. Many people consider **suicide** at some point in their lives. Talking about it can help prevent it. Do your friends a favor and bring the subject out in the open.

Be alert to the possibility of suicide among students you know. Most people give clues when they are considering suicide. Some say it directly. Others hint through offhand comments: "I just don't feel like living any more" or "I can't go on for much longer."

Watch for changes in behavior—withdrawal from social activities, sudden mood swings, inactivity, giving possessions away, or loss of interest in school and friends. When someone is suddenly very calm, even happy, after severe depression, it may indicate that she has chosen suicide. Also, if she has told you she has a plan, and what the plan is, take her at her word.

People who seriously consider killing themselves see suicide as the only solution to painful feelings. They often feel isolated and desperate.

When someone tries to end his life, he is likely to make another attempt. Attempting suicide isn't something he will try once and get out of his system. If you're around someone who is a suicide risk, listen actively. Talk calmly and directly about his suicidal thoughts. Ask him to wait a while before making a decision. Some key things to say are;

"This hard time will pass."
"You can survive these
    painful feelings."
"There are other options."
"You aren't alone."
"Help is nearby."

Most importantly get an adult involved, even if you've been sworn to secrecy. Tell her that you know someone who is talking about suicide. Listen to suicide talk and take it seriously. For more help, look in the phone book or dial the operator and ask for a crisis counseling or suicide hotline.

WORKBOOK
JOURNAL 8-13

# Be Clear About
# Alcohol
# and Other
# Chemicals

## DRUGS HAVE A WAY WITH PEOPLE

Drugs that cause feelings of pleasure or that change people's moods fit roughly into three groups: downers, such as alcohol and tranquilizers; uppers, like cocaine and amphetamines; and psychedelics, such as LSD.

Alcohol, tobacco, marijuana, cocaine, morphine, heroin, LSD, and other chemicals can cause severe damage to people and their families. When people are drunk, high, or stoned, they are chemically impaired. They can get hurt because they trip and fall, burn themselves, have car wrecks, get into fights, are sexually attacked, or are beaten up and robbed.

Many chemicals are also dangerous because they are addictive. When people take them for a while, they are hooked. When they decide to stop using, they can't. The drug has taken over their ability to choose. It takes control of their bodies and their money. Some drugs, crack cocaine, for instance, are so addictive that a user will begin to crave them as soon as they get over their first high.

HUMAN BEINGS have always had the desire to alter their body chemistry. It's strange that we would want to do this artificially. We have a "pharmacy within"—a rich supply of chemicals that produce pleasure or block pain.

Your body makes a form of pain killer that is 200 to 2,000 times more potent than injectable morphine. When you're excited, a powerful drug called adrenaline floods your body and gives you energy. Exercise unleashes other chemicals —endorphins— that help produce "runner's high."

Marijuana has powerful effects on concentration and short-term memory. Focusing on school, homework, or even conversations can be impossible.

You don't have to be a back-alley addict or a sleeping-on-the-sidewalk drunk to be in trouble with drugs. Drinking and drugging have special consequences for teenagers. You could get arrested or worse, depending on the substance.

## PAY ATTENTION

Often people who use drugs don't see what they're doing. It seems like fun, and "everyone else is doing it." One path to stopping the cycle of abuse and addiction is simply to stay alert and observe yourself carefully.

## TELL THE TRUTH

People who have the most serious drug problems are usually the last ones to

## EFFECTS CAN BE PERMANENT

The human brain continues developing until age twenty-one, and the use of controlled substances can affect its growth and maturation. Teenagers who use drugs risk having permanent problems. Alcohol abuse can physically damage the brain and major organ systems. Binge drinking—having several beers or drinks one right after another—will at least make a person sick. It can also cause alcohol poisoning and death.

Pregnant women who drink alcohol can do great harm to their unborn babies. The mental and physical damage that results is called fetal alcohol syndrome (FAS).

admit it. They have excuse after excuse for their behavior: "I'll stop drinking when my father stops bugging me." "Teachers get me uptight. I need to smoke a joint to unwind." "Everybody experiments with drugs a little."

It's funny how reasonable this sounds. The user shifts the blame to everyone and everything outside himself.

If alcohol or other drugs are creating problems in your life, you can end those problems forever: Tell the truth. Admit that your use is getting in the way. When you tell the truth, you begin the process of changing your habit.

## ASK FOR HELP

When you admit that you have been defeated by a chemical, you are free to ask for help. There are many sources of help—friends, parents, teachers, clergy, school counselors, treatment programs, anonymous groups, and more. When you surrender, you win. Admitting that you can't handle the problem alone makes room for other people to assist.

## LOOK OUT FOR YOUR FRIENDS AND FAMILY

You may know people who are in trouble with alcohol or some other chemical. Saying something to them about it can be tricky. You might fear losing a friend or getting put down. If the person in trouble is a parent or another adult, you might be afraid of getting punished or even hurt. However, looking out for each other is worth it. We are all in this life together.

Think carefully about what you'll say to an addicted person. Your message can have more impact if you follow some of these suggestions:

Choose a time when the other person is feeling some regret over chemical use.

Say only what you observe. For example, "Yesterday I smelled alcohol on your breath. I also saw you sleeping in French class."

Show that you care. Avoid judgment. Don't try to lecture, shame, or scare the other person into changing.

State your concern and ask the other person to take the next step: "I'm worried about you. Your drinking is hurting our friendship. Please get help now." If you're worried about your physical safety after saying this, don't be alone with the person.

Suggest sources of help. Your school may have a drug abuse program. Almost every school has a counselor or caring teacher who can help.

Give it time. Don't be surprised if the other person walks away from you, denies the problem, or gets angry at you. Expect it. Allow time for your message to sink in. It may take several attempts.

Leave it alone for a while. You've done what you can do. Now it's up to the other person to change. In the meantime, take care of yourself.

Get support. Share your experiences with others in similar situations and listen to their stories. It can really help. Ask a school counselor about this kind of support group.

## DEAL WITH PEER PRESSURE

Friends who smoke or drink or use other drugs want company. They need to convince themselves that using chemicals is really OK. If you do it too, they might feel better. You don't owe anyone this favor, even if you are made fun of for saying "no." You can turn down the drug without passing judgment on the other person.

Here are some statements you might hear and what you can say back:

*"Oh come on, this stuff really feels good."*

"Yeah, and I know what I'll feel like tomorrow."

*"Adults do this stuff all the time, why can't we?"*

"I can wait until I'm older to decide."

*"Drinking is so cool."*

"I saw someone pass out in his own puke. Cool, huh!"

*"Everyone does it. It doesn't hurt them."*

"How do *you* know?"

*"Man, you are really uptight!"*

"Right now you sound kind of uptight yourself."

*"This stuff isn't all that expensive."*

"It's more than I can afford. Besides, I don't have to spend money to have a great time."

WORKBOOK PRACTICE 8-14

WORKBOOK JOURNAL 8-15

WORKBOOK KEY WORDS

WORKBOOK OUTLINE

WORKBOOK PROGRESS CHECK

# For HELP Call:

## NATIONAL YOUTH CRISIS HOTLINE
A 24-hour phone line that provides help, information and referrals for **any** issue.

1-800-HIT HOME (448-4663)

## TEEN HOTLINE
This phone line is staffed by adults and teens from 12 noon to 12 midnight, Central Standard Time. Call to talk about **any** problem or just to talk.

1-800-522-8336

## NATIONAL RUN AWAY SWITCHBOARD
This 24-hour hotline is for children and teenagers who may be thinking about running away, as well as for those who are already on the street. Callers can be assisted to find help, a shelter, send a message home, or connect a phone call home. (THIS IS ALSO A SUICIDE PREVENTION HOTLINE.)

1-800-621-4000

## AL-ANON AND ALA-TEEN
A support group for people who have a family member or friend with a drug or alcohol problem. Call this number to find a meeting in your area.

1-800-356-9996

## NATIONAL CLEARINGHOUSE FOR ALCOHOL AND DRUG INFORMATION
Call to receive written information on drugs and alcohol.

1-800-SAY NO TO (729-6686)

## ALCOHOL ABUSE AND DRUG HOTLINE
This phone line is staffed 24-hours, providing help, information, and referrals.

1-800-ALCOHOL (252-6465)

## CENTER FOR DISEASE CONTROL NATIONAL AIDS HOTLINE
Call this number 24 hours a day to get help, information, and referrals.

1-800-342-AIDS (2437)
1-800-344-7432 (Spanish speaking,
        8 AM - 2 AM Eastern time)
1-800-243-7889 (TTY, 10 AM -
        10 PM Eastern time)

## CENTER FOR DISEASE CONTROL NATIONAL STD (SEXUALLY TRANSMITTED DISEASES) HOTLINE
Call this number 24 hours a day to get help, information, and referrals.

1-800-227-8922 (Monday-Friday,
        8 AM - 11 PM, Eastern time)

## AMERICAN ANOREXIA/ BULIMIA ASSOCIATION
This organization provides help and referrals for anyone with an eating disorder.

1-212-501-8351 (Monday-Friday,
9 AM - 5 PM, Eastern time)

# Chapter 9 Objectives

After mastering this chapter you will be able to:

- USE A FIVE-STEP PROCESS FOR WRITING

- PRODUCE A QUALITY TERM PAPER

# CHAPTER WRITE 9

# Write for the J☺y of It

THIS CHAPTER is about writing more effectively and quickly and with more pleasure. It might be a term paper, an answer to an essay question, or a homework assignment. It might be writing an essay, a letter to a friend, or an entry in your diary. Whatever your purpose, you can use the tips in this chapter to produce better writing, in less time.

If writing isn't one of your favorite things, consider the choice you have right now. You could decide just to go through the motions and get through this chapter without really working at it. If you do, your feelings about writing will stay the same as they are now. But, if you really commit to practicing a new approach, you could totally change your experience of writing.

This chapter presents a complete writing process that you can use as is, or modify to suit yourself. Even if you do create your own process, start with the one explained in this chapter. It may show you some new methods.

You may be wondering just how much time and energy this will take. Here's the answer: To learn the new process, write one 250-word essay. That's just two handwritten pages or one typed page. Invest three hours in this effort, using the simple instructions in this chapter, and you could save much more than that on your very next writing assignment.

The writing process can be broken down into six easy steps:

1. Plan
2. Brainstorm
3. Organize
4. Pick a topic
5. Draft
6. Revise and edit

WORKBOOK PRACTICE 9-1

WORKBOOK JOURNAL 9-2

# Plan Your Paper

**G**REAT PAPERS START with a **plan**, the first step in our writing process. In planning an essay, you specify:

Topic
Purpose
Audience
Specific requirements

**TOPIC**—Depending upon your teacher, the **topic** may be assigned or it may be your choice.

**PURPOSE**—When it comes to writing, you can have more than one **purpose**. Your first purpose may be to get a good grade. A second purpose might be to create a quality essay. Other purposes might be to:

Inform readers
Interest readers in something new
Change your readers' minds
    about an issue
Persuade readers to take
    some action
Amuse or entertain your readers

Here are some examples:
When writing a lab report for biology, you might want to inform readers about your observations. In American government class, you may write to convince lawmakers to increase taxes so there will be more money for schools.

In a book report, your first purpose might be to inform readers about the main ideas in a particular book, and your secondary purpose might be to amuse your readers and convince them to read the book.

**AUDIENCE**—Your audience can include your teacher or anyone else who may have an interest in your subject.

**SPECIFIC REQUIREMENT**—You may be asked to write a paper of a certain length, either by page count or number of words. It may be necessary to follow certain rules of style, such as how sources are identified. You may be required to submit your paper in type-written form.

WORKBOOK PRACTICE 9-3

# Brainstorm Ideas

ONCE YOU HAVE DONE your planning, **brainstorming** is a powerful way to overcome procrastination, untangle confusion, and figure out what you want to say. Brainstorming works best when you just let your mind roam. Write down whatever comes to you. There's no need to evaluate your thoughts.

## KEY WORDS

One way to brainstorm is to think of Key Words. A key word describes a main idea or thought. Here are some techniques to get you started:

1. Write the topic of your essay at the top of a blank sheet of paper.

2. Relax. Get comfortable. Close your eyes or look out the window. Take a few deep breaths and let the tension in your muscles melt away.

3. Create an image in your mind that relates to your topic. Write down any word or phrase that describes the image. As the next thought or image comes to mind, write words that describe it. Continue jotting down these Key Words, describing people, places, things, and ideas you might include in your essay.

A list of Key Words brainstormed for an essay on the topic of "My Summer Vacation" might look like this:

My Summer Vacation (Key Words)
worked
water-skiing
northern Minnesota
resort
swimming
cleaned cabins
made donuts
lakes
waited tables
slalom
fishing
ten-pound walleye
camping
movies
mosquitoes

## KEY SENTENCES

Once you have your Key Words listed, you can create Key Sentences. These fill in details about the Key Words you brainstormed. This is not a first draft of your paper. It is just a list of sentences covering the main ideas for your essay.

Write out your Key Sentences quickly, in any order. Don't worry about spelling, punctuation, or grammar. Incomplete sentences and phrases are OK for now. When you've captured a particular idea in a single Key Sentence, move on to a new one.

Keep generating Key Sentences until you've covered the points and ideas suggested by your Key Words. Depending upon the length of the composition, that might be five to fifteen sentences. You might want to check off each Key Word as you use it in a Key Sentence. Also, cross out Key Words for any ideas or facts that you decide to leave out.

Following are Key Sentences to go with the Key Words about "My Summer Vacation." Note that the sentences were not written in any special order.

*My Summer Vacation*
  (Key Sentences)

I worked at a resort in northern Minnesota.

Cleaning cabins and waiting tables was more fun than I thought.

I helped make the doughnuts in the morning.

I went water-skiing a lot.

The resort is on a big lake.

The mosquitoes were terrible.

I went camping and fishing with my friends.

I saw a lot of movies at the dollar theater.

I learned how to slalom ski.

I caught a ten-pound walleye.

WORKBOOK PRACTICE 9-4

# Organize

ORGANIZING INVOLVES clustering or grouping your ideas and putting them in an order or sequence. List your Key Words as before, then gather them into clusters related to the same topic.

Suppose you want to write an essay about the airlines. Your list of Key Words could include:

airlines
flight attendant service
expansion plans
waiting lines
airline food
airport parking
late departures
small seats
noisy planes
too many planes
regional airports
buses to airport

Cluster the Key Words around topics like this:

Topic: airport problems
Keywords: waiting line
            airport parking
            noisy planes
            too many planes

Topic: solutions
Keywords: expansion plans
            regional airports
            buses to airport

Topic: in-flight problems
Keywords: airline food
            late departures
            small seats

Each cluster of words would then form one section of the essay. Number the clusters in a logical order, and guess what—you're organized.

Another way to **organize** your writing is to use Key Sentences. Decide which idea comes first, which comes second, and so on. Then put a number next to each sentence.

When you're finished numbering, read the Key Sentences in order and decide whether this arrangement makes sense. If not, cross out the numbers and change the order. Ordering is a left-brain process that involves numbers and logic.

Although there are many ways of ordering information, the following approaches can be useful.

### 1. CHRONOLOGICAL ORDER

Describe events in the time sequence in which they occurred. Novels, plays, short stories, and history books are often organized this way.

### 2. LOCATION OR POSITION

Describe things based on their location or the order in which you encounter them. In a book report, for example, you might write about each of the chapters in the order they occurred in the book. In a paper on astronomy, you could discuss the planets in order of their distance from the sun.

### 3. INTRODUCTION, DESCRIPTION/ANALYSIS, CONCLUSION

Start by introducing an issue or posing a problem to solve. Then analyze the issue, discussing the facts and ideas involved. Finally, recommend a course of action or draw a conclusion. Sometimes your recommendations or conclusions are stated in the introduction.

### 4. OVERVIEW, MAJOR FACTS, MINOR FACTS

To communicate a series of facts or ideas, arrange the items in order of importance. On the topic of drinking and driving, for instance, you might organize the facts like this:

Car crashes involving a drunk person kill many thousands of people in the U.S. each year.

Drinking impairs judgment, motor functions, and vision.

Alcohol awareness and driver education programs are helping reduce incidents of drunk driving.

Most states consider a 0.10% blood alcohol level to be evidence of intoxication.

WORKBOOK PRACTICE 9-5

WORKBOOK PRACTICE 9-6

WORKBOOK PRACTICE 9-7

# Pick a Topic

W HEN IT'S TIME to choose a topic for an essay, this list can be a starting place. These items are only general ideas. Use brainstorming to turn one of them into a more specific topic for your writing.

Something I Feel Happy About (or Sad, Fearful, or Angry About)

What My Father (or Mother, Sister, Brother, Grandfather, Grandmother) Taught Me

The Job I Have (or Had)

One of My Goals

A Conflict in My Life

An Experience That Taught Me Something

A Holiday Celebration at My Home

My Bedroom

My Favorite: Food, Clothes, Sport, Movie, TV Show, Book, Magazine, Teacher, Memory, Music Group

My Pet

A Unique Person I Know

A Special Gift

Something I: Want to Learn, Have Been Putting Off, Am Proud Of, Am Good At

If I Had $5,000 to Spend As I Want

What I Want to Be When I Grow Up

An Issue That I Feel Strongly About

A Problem in America

Answering Machines

Fashion

Hairstyles

UFO's

Smoking

# Draft

After planning, brainstorming, and organizing, you're ready for your first **draft**. A first draft is a first writing of a composition. As you write, aim to include everything that is consistent with your plan—the facts and figures, dates and times, recommendations and conclusions.

Drafting is a right-brain task. Do it quickly—as quickly as you can write. Ignore the rules of grammar, spelling, punctuation, and capitalization. Just get the words down, then get it right. By saving the editing for later, you can produce better work in less time

# Exercise

*Plan, brainstorm, organize, and draft an essay of about 250 words. You may pick any topic. In order to focus on the new writing process, it is probably best to choose some familiar topic.*

## USE PROOFREADERS' MARKS

When editing you can save time by using special symbols called proofreader's marks. These symbols are used by editors, teachers, and secretaries to quickly indicate text changes.

Study the chart of proofreader's marks for a few minutes to see what they mean. There are editing exercises in *The Learning Power Workbook* in which you practice using proofreader's marks.

| Margin Mark | Meaning and Text Marking |
|---|---|
| ⌐ᶥor ᶥ⌐or ᵞ | ~~Delete~~ (take out) |
| ◠ | Clos̆e up |
| **stet** | Leave as ~~printed~~ (when matter has been crossed out by mistake) |
| **caps** | Change to <u>capital</u> letters |
| *lc* | Change capitals to /lower case |
| ∧ | Insert (or substitute) comma |
| ⊙ | Insert (or substitute) period |
| # | Insert space |
| ⟟R | Transpose items these |
| )[ | Center |
| ¶ | Begin new paragraph |
| ∧ | (caret mark) Insert matter indicated in margin |
| ⱽ ⱽ | Insert double quotes |
| ⱽ | Insert apostrophe or single quote |

WORKBOOK PRACTICE 9-8

# Revise and Edit

A LMOST NO ONE produces finished copy on the first try. Professional writers usually write a rough draft and then revise it and edit it several times. When editing *A Farewell to Arms*, Hemingway rewrote the ending 39 times.

In this book the words *revise* and *edit* stand for two separate steps in the overall editing of a rough draft. Revising means checking the content and sequence of your writing. At this step you add, delete, and rearrange sentences and paragraphs.

When you are satisfied with your revisions, you edit, checking for grammar, spelling, and style, sentence by sentence and word by word.

## REVISE

To revise a draft, read it while paying attention to:

Sequence
Completeness
Accuracy
Logic

If possible, ask someone else to read your work and give you comments. Remind them to ignore grammar and spelling. This is still a draft and has not been edited. You may   also find it helpful to read it aloud to yourself or into a tape recorder.

If you find any problems, fix them. Some options are to:

Add sentences and paragraphs that present material omitted in the draft

Delete sentences and paragraphs that are unnecessary or repetitious

Rearrange sentences or paragraphs to make the order more logical or interesting

When you revise, do not recopy the draft. Use proofreaders' marks to indicate additions, deletions, and any rearrangements of sentences and paragraphs.

After you have revised your draft, read it again. Make any additional revisions you find necessary.

# Exercise

*Ask two people to read your draft and give you verbal comments. Take notes on what they say. Make appropriate changes, such as adding, deleting, or rearranging sentences and paragraphs. Do not recopy the essay; use proofreaders' marks instead. Don't worry about editing for spelling, grammar, or style during the revising process.*

## EDIT

Here are four common rules for editing:

1. USE COMPLETE SENTENCES
2. DELETE UNNECESSARY WORDS
3. CHECK SPELLINGS AND MEANINGS OF WORDS
4. CHECK GRAMMAR, PUNCTUATION, AND CAPITALIZATION

### 1. USE COMPLETE SENTENCES

The first editing strategy is to make sure that every sentence is complete. A **complete** sentence has at least one subject, one verb, and expresses a complete thought.

In some sentences, however, the subject or verb may be omitted. This is grammatically OK, as long as the omitted word is understood. For example, in commands or requests, the word you is frequently omitted. For example:

"Tell me what time it is, please."

Here the subject—you—is understood. The sentence means:

"You tell me what time it is, please."

# Exercise

*Examine your revised draft sentence by sentence. Is every sentence complete? If you find one that's not, edit to make it a complete sentence. Use proofreaders' marks.*

## 2. DELETE UNNECESSARY WORDS

Your written work will be clearer if your sentences aren't loaded with extra words. Some teachers prefer long sentences; others suggest you keep them short. Teachers almost always disapprove of words that don't add to the meaning.

To find and delete unnecessary words, edit sentence by sentence. First, read a sentence to find out what it says. Then strike out as many words as possible without losing any meaning:

*History is usually thought of as a record of what has happened in the past.*

After deleting some words, we have:

*History is usually thought of as a record of the past.*

This rewrite above means the same as the original, but it is shorter and clearer. Both sentences are grammatically correct. However, meaning gets lost if you delete too many words:

*History is the past.*

# Exercise

*Edit your draft by deleting unnecessary words.*

WORKBOOK
PRACTICE 9-11

### 3. CHECK SPELLINGS AND MEANINGS OF WORDS

Accurate spelling is essential when writing magazines and books, business reports and letters, and assignments in schools and colleges. Whether or not you agree, people will judge your spelling against accepted standards.

Using words properly is as important as spelling. Sometimes we misuse a word because we mistake its meaning. At other times, we mistake one word for another that sounds similar. For example, these pairs of words are often confused:

affect / effect
then / than
their / they're
your / you're
to / too
stationery / stationary

In the above list, all the words are spelled correctly; even a spell check program on a computer won't find these errors. So watch out for word meaning, and keep an eye out for slang. Use slang only when writing dialogue. Slang includes words such as:

| | |
|---|---|
| ain't | cuz |
| cool | dude |
| dis or dissed | crib |

# Exercise

*Use your partially edited essay for this exercise. If you are using a computer, spell check your essay first. Then, with or without a computer, examine each word in your essay. If you are uncertain of a word's meaning or spelling, check it in your dictionary. Make any necessary corrections.*

WORKBOOK PRACTICE 9-12

WORKBOOK PRACTICE 9-13

## 4. Check Grammar, Punctuation, and Capitalization

Some of the **grammar** we use in everyday speech is not used in writing. Our own sense of what is or is not acceptable may not always be correct. For that reason, using a reference book to check grammar, punctuation, and capitalization is essential.

Professional editors commonly use grammar and style references and dictionaries as they work. The rest of us can benefit from doing the same.

Two excellent grammar references are available in paperback for around $5: *Write Right*, by Jan Vanolia, published by Ten Speed Press; and *Elements of Style*, by Strunk and White, published by Macmillan.

# Exercise

*Examine the grammar and punctuation of each sentence in your essay. If you find any errors, correct them. If you are uncertain about anything, consult a grammar reference or your teacher.*

WORKBOOK PRACTICE 9-14

# Revisit the Writing Process

**PLAN**
Topic
Purpose
Audience
Specific requirements

**BRAINSTORM**
Jot down Key Words

**ORGANIZE**
Jot down Key Sentences or
cluster Key Words

Number Key Sentences or clusters
in logical order

> Chronological order
>
> Location or position
>
> Introduction,
> description/analysis,
> conclusion
>
> Overview, major facts,
> minor facts

**PICK A TOPIC**

**DRAFT**

**REVISE AND EDIT**
Use complete sentences
Delete unnecessary words
Check spellings and meanings
of words
Check grammar, punctuation,
and capitalization

WORKBOOK
PRACTICE 9-15

# Using the Writing Process During Tests

FACED WITH A TIME LIMIT, many students are tempted to dive into essay tests without a plan. They crank out words like mad, afraid to reread their answers, hoping they will somehow sound OK in the end.

Use the writing process explained in this chapter to save time and to help you record your thinking in a first-class way.

Essay test questions reveal the topic you are to write about and give you hints for defining your purpose. Look for Key Words such as:

define
identify
list
describe
discuss
review
summarize
outline
compare
contrast
analyze
demonstrate
show
support
 criticize
assess
comment
evaluate

Once you're clear about your topic and purpose, brainstorm as many ideas as you can. Use Key Words and Key Sentences or clustering to organize the ideas. If you run out of time, having just the Key Sentences written down may get you partial credit.

After you finish writing your answer, read it over and correct any mistakes. Use a pen or pencil that writes clearly, and practice your best penmanship.

# Engage Both Sides of Your Brain

THE HUMAN BRAIN is divided into two hemispheres, right and left. The two halves typically work together. Still, some tasks tend to be **right-brain** tasks and others **left-brain** tasks. The writing process involves both sides of your brain. Right-brain tasks are more creative and intuitive. Left-brain tasks are more logical and analytical.

These brain functions may be reversed or mixed in a small percentage of people. In general:

A person with a blood clot in the left hemisphere will have paralysis of the right arm and leg and difficulty speaking.

A person with a blood clot in the right hemisphere will have paralysis of the left arm and leg, but generally no difficulty with speech.

**RIGHT BRAIN**
*Controls left arm and leg*
*Controls rhythm*
*Looks at the whole*
*Responds to images*
*Notices emotions*

**LEFT BRAIN**
*Controls right arm and leg*
*Controls speech*
*Notices details*
*Thinks logically*
*Processes facts and rules*

Some steps in the writing process are analytical, left-brain tasks. Others are creative, right-brain tasks. Both types of thinking are necessary—but not always at the same time. For example, when you start writing, it pays to plan first. That's a left-brain task. Then you can use brain-storming, which is a right-brain, creative task. Writing a first draft is predominately a right-brain activity.

WORKBOOK PRACTICE 9-16

# Write Legibly

E WILL WRITE with computers more and more, but there are times when it is necessary, convenient, or merely desirable to write in longhand. It's important that your penmanship be **legible** to your reader. When you take notes in school, you are the intended reader. When you take a test, your intended reader is your teacher. Both you and your teacher need to be able to read and understand your handwriting.

To improve your handwriting, bring your attention to how you are forming each letter, just as you did when you were first learning to print or write longhand. Just watching yourself form letters will begin immediately to improve your penmanship.

WORKBOOK
PRACTICE 9-17

# Finish a Term Paper in 10 Steps

**T**ERM PAPER ASSIGNMENTS require planning, time management, research, note taking, organizing, problem solving, and writing skills. In short, successfully completing a term paper assignment involves nearly all your study skills.

Learning to prepare a term paper offers many benefits. You learn how to find information and organize facts and ideas. You work independently outside of the classroom, just as you might be expected to do when you are employed. And writing a paper is a powerful way to communicate your ideas.

Large writing assignments can seem overwhelming. When you feel overwhelmed, take refuge in planning and spreading the necessary steps out over time. It's possible to stay up all night and finish a paper—and even get a good grade. But this is tiring and stressful, and it won't win you consistently higher grades.

A saner alternative is to write the paper using these steps:

1. Choose a topic
2. Look it up in a dictionary
3. Look it up in an encyclopedia
4. Narrow your topic
5. Look up the topic in reference materials
6. Take notes
7. Write a thesis statement
8. Organize the paper
9. Draft
10. Revise and edit

## 1. CHOOSE A TOPIC
Instructors often ask you to choose a topic for your paper. In the beginning, a general topic will do. If you have difficulty, start with a chapter title from your textbook. Pick the subject that's most interesting to you.

## 2. LOOK IT UP IN A DICTIONARY
A dictionary may give you a better understanding of your topic. Look for meanings you don't know. Write down the meanings on note cards and look at the cards over a period of several days. Write down any questions about the topic as they occur to you.

### 3. Look It Up in an Encyclopedia

Look up the Key Words in your topic, seeking to answer your questions. Write the main points on note cards. At this point you may know quite a bit about your topic.

### 4. Narrow Your Topic

It is important to narrow your topic to make it manageable. Ask yourself questions about it. If you start with medicine, for example, do you want to write about doctors or patients? If your answer is patients, do you want to write about getting well or getting sick? If you choose getting sick, what diseases are you interested in learning about? If the answer is cancer, what kind? Are you interested in treatments or symptoms of the disease? Each time you answer, you narrow the topic further. You also develop questions for your paper.

### 5. Look Up Your Topic in Reference Manuals

Use **periodicals**, reference books, and books from the library stacks to do research on your topic. Search until you find several books, articles, or other materials that give you a lot of information about your subject. You'll probably read more information than you will actually use.

### 6. Take Notes

Take notes on note cards. Number and title the note cards so you can organize them, and keep cards with similar information together. Highlight the key ideas, names, and facts on your cards.

On each card include the basics: the author's name, the source (book, article, tape) that you're working from, and the page number. You can also make separate note cards for your original ideas.

When taking notes, you have two choices: (1) to **paraphrase** the author in your own words or (2) to **quote the author** directly. Put quotation marks around passages you quote exactly, and remember to credit the source of quotes or paraphrased statements.

### 7. Write a Thesis Statement

Now is an appropriate time to define the purpose of your paper. Term papers commonly prove or disprove a **thesis**. A thesis is a statement of theory or opinion. Another word for thesis is hypothesis. Often the thesis statement answers a question, such as "Does smoking cause cancer?"

Keep in mind the difference between a topic and a thesis statement. A topic simply names an area of knowledge, such as:

*Space and medicine*
*Rock music*
*Religion*

A thesis statement, in contrast, says something about the topic. Thesis statements are complete sentences:

*Space exploration has changed medicine.*

*A primary attraction of rock music is that it's different from past music.*

*War is often a product of religious differences.*

## 8. ORGANIZE THE PAPER
Start by putting away your note cards. Take out a clean sheet of paper and brainstorm Key Words. Use Clustering, or Key Sentences, to organize the paper. Then go over your note cards to see if you forgot any major points.

## 9. DRAFT
Referring to your outline, quickly write a draft. There's no need to worry about grammar, punctuation, or spelling. Your purpose for now is to present the ideas, facts, and figures that will explain and support your thesis.

## 10. REVISE AND EDIT
Use the revise and edit steps in the writing process, as explained in this chapter. Read your draft aloud and note paragraphs that need revising or rearranging. If you are missing some important facts, go back to your reference materials and fill in the gaps. When the paragraphs are in order and you think the relevant points are covered, edit sentence by sentence. If possible, ask a friend or instructor to give you comments. Then revise and edit again.

WORKBOOK PRACTICE 9-18
WORKBOOK PRACTICE 9-19
WORKBOOK PRACTICE 9-20

# Avoid Plagiarism

P LAGIARISM IS A KIND of cheating. To plagiarize means to present someone else's work as your own. It usually applies to writing. An example is when someone copies an article from the encyclopedia word for word and presents it as his own writing.

**Plagiarism** can have serious consequences. You could be expelled from school, receive a failing grade, be embarrassed, or even be sued.

Often plagiarism is deliberate, but even honest students can plagiarize by accident. You can avoid this fate by adopting the following writing habits.

## QUOTE SOURCES EXACTLY

When reading background materials, decide which passages you want to quote word for word. Copy those passages down exactly as they appear in the original source. Enclose each of these passages in quotation marks (" "). Then you'll know which words are your own creation and which are the creation of someone else.

> In Portugal "avoid making business appointments between noon and 3pm when everything closes down."
>
> Do's and Taboos Around the World, 2nd ed.
> Roger E. Axtell, Editor
> © 1990
> page 65

In addition, list the source of each quote. Include the title, author, and publication date of the book or article.

## SUMMARIZE CAREFULLY

Instead of quoting a source, you may sum up a passage in your own words. But you must use your words—not the author's to summarize. Read the original passage and ask yourself, "What's the main point here?" Then express that point in a sentence or two, as if you were explaining it to someone else.

## CREDIT SOURCES FAIRLY

In your final paper, list all the sources for passages you quote. Typically you do this with footnotes or a bibliography. Your teacher can explain how. This step will be easy if you keep track of your sources and summarize carefully.

WORKBOOK PRACTICE 9-21

# Cook Up Some Instant Poetry

**W**RITING POETRY is a great way to express your thoughts and feelings. It can also improve your writing skill.

You don't have to enforce a rhyming scheme on a series of words to make a poem. Poetry can be memorable without strict meter or rhyme. Poetry is concentrated, musical language. You can create this "music" by "listening" for the rhythm and sound of words and phrases.

As a way to get started, try experimenting with these techniques:

Begin each line with a repeated phrase, such as "I knew her when . . . " or "I remember . . . "

Choose a common subject for each line. For example, in each line, mention the name of someone you know and the one thing that comes to mind about that person.

Make simple lists. Almost any list will do—the objects you see in a room, the people you see in a public area, the flowers you see in a garden. Include specific, concrete details that appeal to your senses.

Then include in your poem what this list reveals about the people or events involved.

If you think you might enjoy writing poetry, read the work of great poets from various cultures. Reading mixed with writing practice is a quick recipe for instant poetry.

WORKBOOK
JOURNAL 9-22

# WRITE For Personal Reasons

**Y**OUR PERSONAL LIFE will be richer if you learn to write well. Here are some of the ways that skill in writing can serve you during your lifetime:

## INFLUENCE PUBLIC OPINION

Persuade others by writing to the editor of your local newspaper or your favorite magazines.

## CHANGE GOVERNMENT POLICY

Help shape new laws. Your elected representatives are paid to listen to you and to read and respond to your letters.

## COMPLAIN ABOUT PRODUCTS AND SERVICES

A brief letter of complaint, detailing the time and location of the purchase and the exact problem or defect, can help to quickly resolve your issue and may get you a refund.

## CLARIFY PERSONAL OPTIONS

When you're stuck on a problem, put all the solutions you can think of in writing. Later, when you're "unstuck," write about the option you chose, how well it worked, and what you could do differently next time.

## THANK PEOPLE

Thank-you notes and letters of appreciation can go a long way in building and maintaining your relationships. Thoughtfulness expressed in writing has enduring and endearing value.

## RESOLVE CONFLICTS

It can be much easier to frame your thoughts and feelings in writing before you try to express them face to face. At times it may be very effective to write to someone instead of speaking with him.

## SET GOALS

Describe what you'd like to have, do, or be tomorrow, next month, next year, or in five, ten or twenty years.

## KEEP A JOURNAL

Imagine a friend who's available twenty-four hours a day, ready to listen to and reflect on your thoughts and feelings. That friend can be your journal.

WORKBOOK PRACTICE 9-23    WORKBOOK JOURNAL 9-24    WORKBOOK KEY WORDS    WORKBOOK OUTLINE    WORKBOOK PROGRESS CHECK

# Chapter 10 Objectives

After mastering this chapter you will be able to:

- TAKE AN EXPERIMENTAL APPROACH TO MATH

- SIMPLIFY WORD PROBLEMS

- COMPUTE YOUR COURSE GRADES

# CHAPTER MATH MATTERS

# Solve Problems Like a Mathematician

**M**ANY STUDENTS feel stuck if they can't figure out how to solve a math problem the minute they look at it. It might help to know that mathematicians don't always know how to find the answers to problems they face, either.

A mathematician chooses a method she thinks might work and tries it. Her first approach might work, and it might not. She knows that trial and error is part of problem solving. She learns to check her own work and to catch her errors.

Learning to solve math problems involves dozens of techniques. Some of them are:

| | |
|---|---|
| adding | dividing |
| graphing | subtracting |
| estimating | using fractions |
| multiplying | measuring |
| factoring | |

These techniques, and others, are your tools. Most math courses are concerned with learning about these tools and how to use them to solve problems.

Mathematicians are like detectives. They investigate, gather clues, test evidence, and identify suspects. They sort through their math tools, looking for one that will fit the problem. You can do this too. Solving math problems becomes easier and faster as you sharpen your skills through practice.

WORKBOOK
JOURNAL 10-1

WORKBOOK
PRACTICE 10-2

# Do the
# **Logical**
# Calculation

**S**UPPOSE YOU and a friend get a job cleaning up Mr. Perez's yard. He pays you both a total of $12. If you split it equally, how much does each of you get? Obviously, $6. How did you solve this problem? You may have thought:

"We each get half.
$12 divided by two is $6."

Or you might have thought:

"We each get half.
$12 times one-half is $6 each."

How did you know whether to multiply or divide? And how did you know what numbers to use? You probably didn't use a formula. Instead, you just did the **logical calculation**, the one that made sense.

Mathematicians solve problems using logic, just as you did in the example above. Learning to tell for yourself what is logical and what isn't is a key to solving math problems. Do what makes sense. Then ask, "Can this answer possibly be right?"

WORKBOOK
PRACTICE 10-3

# Simplify the Pro·blem

IT'S GREAT WHEN YOU see an obvious, logical way to solve a problem. Unfortunately, it is not always that easy. Some problems are tough to solve. You may be presented with so much information that you get confused. You suspect that a problem will require several steps, but you don't know which comes first.

To simplify a problem, put it into your own words, separate useful from useless information, and break it down into manageable parts.

Here's an example:

Mom asks you to walk 5 blocks to Vinnie's Corner Grocery. She wants you to buy dog food, which is on sale for $6.19. She hands you a $10 bill and says she wants either as many quarters or as many dimes as she can possibly get back in change so she can go to the laundromat. The sales tax rate is 4%. How many dimes or quarters does Mom get when you return home? (She expects all her change back.)

You could start on this problem by translating it into your own words. One student said it like this:

"Mom is weird. She wants all of her change back in either quarters or dimes. I'm not sure which. First, I have to figure out how much the tax will be."

When you use your own language to describe the problem, you make it seem more familiar and real. Putting a problem in your own words enables you to solve it on your own terms. You also begin to pick out the information you need in order to solve it.

The fact that you have to walk five blocks to Vinnie's is useless information for this problem because it doesn't affect how much change you will get back. Why would a problem contain useless information? It helps you practice being a critical thinker.

Much of the information you will receive throughout your life will be useless. Learning to pick out what's important will help you in school, in your personal matters, and in your future occupation.

What is the important information in the dog food problem? Since the question is about how much change you get back, it is important to know the price of the item ($6.19), the tax rate (4%), and how much money you give the cashier ($10). Don't forget that Mom wants either all dimes or all quarters.

After you decide what is important, you can break the problem down into workable chunks. The first job is to calculate what the total cost will be. The price of the dog food is $6.19, and tax is 4%. Four percent is the same as 0.04.

($6.19)(0.04) = $0.2476.
Round this off to the nearest penny.
The tax is 25 cents.
$6.19 + $0.25 = $6.44
The total cost including tax is $6.44.

You hand the cashier $10, and you get $3.56 back.

$10.00
−$ 6.44
$ 3.56

Now let's get to the quarters and dimes. Since the problem says the change is to be in either dimes *or* quarters, there are two solutions. If the dimes and quarters seem confusing, create a similar, but simpler, problem.

For example, if you were getting only $1 back, it could be either four quarters or ten dimes. You get the answer by multiplying the $1 by either four or ten.

Apply the same logic to this problem. Here you're getting $3.56 back. Multiplying by four, to get quarters, you get 14.24 *quarters*. Multiplying by ten, to get dimes, you get 35.6 *dimes*.

4 quarters x 3.56 dollars
= 14.24 quarters

10 dimes x 3.56 dollars
= 35.6 dimes

It is very important to see that the answers are expressed in quarters or dimes, not in dollars and cents. Since we can't easily divide up a quarter or a dime, we take the 14 whole quarters or 35 whole dimes, and we convert the rest of the change into cents.

0.24 X 0.25 dollars = 0.06 dollars
= $ .06

0.6 X 0.1 dollars = 0.06 dollars
=$ .06

0.24 *quarters* and 0.6 *dimes* are the same as 0.06 dollars or 6 cents.

Finally, check your answer. Does it make sense? In the above example, if you brought back quarters, multiply the 14 quarters by $0.25. The answer is $3.50, which, along with the extra $ .06, is the amount of change you were to get back. If you brought home dimes, multiply 35 dimes by $0.10. The result, again, is $3.50. Don't forget the 6 cents. Mom won't.

# TRY Alternative Methods

**W**HEN YOU ENCOUNTER a problem that lacks a clear-cut approach, try the method that seems most reasonable. Sometimes more than one approach will work. Following is an example that has at least two workable approaches.

Your cooperative learning team is arranging transportation for your class to visit an observatory. You have asked parents to drive, and you have several volunteers lined up, along with their cars and vans. The maximum number of people riding in each car cannot exceed the number of seats with seat belts.

There are three cars with five seats each, one van with eight seats and one with seven seats, and three cars with four seats each. Your class has thirty-one kids. In addition to the parents who are driving, your teacher and an assistant are also going on the trip. Do you need all of these vehicles? Do you need more?

In order to answer these questions, you need to know how many people are riding and how many seats are available.

One method of solving the problem is to find the *total* number of seats available and the *total* number of people riding, including the drivers:

3 cars x 5 seats = 15 seats
1 van x 8 seats = 8 seats
1 van x 7 seats = 7 seats
3 cars x 4 seats = 12 seats

15 seats + 8 seats + 7 seats
+ 12 seats = 42 seats

In order to include the drivers, you must first count the vehicles:

3 cars + 1 van + 1 van + 3 cars = 8 vehicles = 8 drivers.

Now you can determine the total number of riders:

31 kids + 1 teacher + 1 assistant + 8 drivers = 41 total people

There are enough seats with one left over.

Another method of solving the problem is to determine the number of passenger seats that are available in each vehicle. We can do this by taking away one seat in each vehicle for the driver to occupy:

3 cars x 4 passenger seats = 12 passenger seats

1 van x 7 passenger seats = 7 passenger seats

1 van x 6 passenger seats = 6 passenger seats

3 cars x 3 passenger seats = 9 passenger seats

12 + 7 + 6 + 9 = 34 passenger seats available. There are 31 kids plus one teacher and one assistant, or 33 total passengers. Since there are 33 passengers for 34 seats, there are enough vehicles and all the vehicles will be needed.

Notice that in the second approach, counting the total number of vehicles and drivers was never necessary. Either approach works.

# Expand Your
# UNDERSTANDING

WORDS LIKE *ALGEBRA* and *geometry* can strike fear in the hearts of students. It is important to realize that you have the power to master these subjects. Deepening your understanding can make some aspects of math seem more friendly and familiar.

One way to begin understanding math is to think of equations as sentences in English. As babies we first learn individual words: Mommy, Daddy, eat, TV, hello, and so on. Later we join the words into sentences to express more complex thoughts: "I'll pick you up at your house at noon on Saturday, and we'll go to the mall."

As we become educated, we write whole essays using words and sentences. In some situations a single word or simple sentence will do. But to explain or describe complex thoughts, we use many complex sentences. That's how language develops. An understanding of math develops in a similar manner.

Math is like a foreign language. Translating words and phrases into English may be helpful. Here are examples of equations as sentences:

$(3 \times 4) \div 6 = 2$   Three multiplied by four and divided by six equals two.
$5^2 + 10 = 35$   Five squared plus 10 equals 35.
$4 + y = 9$   Four plus y equals nine.

To be more comfortable with math, become familiar with math's symbols. For example, "3" is a symbol that represents a specific number—three. In algebra you will be introduced to other symbols that stand for numbers. The letters "a" and "b," for instance, are called variables, because their values will vary (change from one problem to the next).

Other common symbols are "x" and "y." These symbols usually represent unknown numbers, the ones you will find out or "solve for" in the problem. For instance, in the equation 7a + x = 20, we could choose to have "a" be the number 2. After we have selected a value for "a," we can solve the equation for the value of the unknown number "x," which equals 6 in this case. Or we can just let "a" be "a" and solve the problem like this:

$$x = 20-7a$$

The important thing to know here is that the symbol "a" can have any value, and the "statement" will still be true.

It might help to think of unknowns ("x", "y", etc.) as question marks. While in arithmetic we use the symbol "x" to stand for multiplication (4 x 6 = 24), in algebra "x" is an unknown. When there may be confusion, we use parentheses rather than "x" to indicate multiplication: (4)(6) = 24.

Once you are familiar with the language of math, you will be on your way to mastering the subject.

# Compute Your Grades

OMPUTING YOUR COURSE grades can help you in several ways. You can find out the value of tests, projects, labs, term papers, homework, and class participation. Knowing how each of these affects your final grade will help you decide what to do to earn the grades you want.

You can also be sure you are getting the highest grade you deserve. Mistakes are sometimes made when calculating grades. By knowing where you stand, you can avoid any big surprises.

Quarter or semester grades are usually based on the grades received on assignments, quizzes, and tests. Each item counts as a certain percentage of your overall grade.

Think of **percentages** as dollars, and you earn a certain number of dollars for each assignment or test that you complete. Say that the highest possible grade at the end of the course is 100%. You could think of this as $100, the maximum that can be earned for the term. If you earn between $90 and $100, you get an "A," from $80 to $89 a "B," and so on.

A quiz or test during the semester may be worth $5, $10, or $20. Each item that counts toward your final grade has a value. Here's an example:

| | | |
|---|---|---|
| Quiz | $5 | (5%) |
| Quiz | $5 | (5%) |
| Quiz | $5 | (5%) |
| Quiz | $5 | (5%) |
| Midterm Exam | $10 | (10%) |
| Final Exam | $25 | (25%) |
| Term Paper | $15 | (15%) |
| Class Participation | $15 | (15%) |
| Homework | $15 | (15%) |
| Total | $100 | (100%) |

The values shown are the most you can earn for each item. Divide your percentage score by 100 to convert it to a decimal, then multiply that number times the amount that is possible to earn for the midterm test ($10). If you get a score of 100% on the midterm, you get the full value of $10.

If your score is 82%, then you earn $8.20.

$$\text{Maximum value} \times \text{Your score} = \text{Amount earned}$$

If the maximum value for a quiz was $5, and you scored 85%, you would multiply these numbers ($5 x 0.85) and get $4.25 as the amount earned. Add the amounts for each item to get your total grade for the class.

| | SCORE | VALUE | COUNTS |
|---|---|---|---|
| Quiz | 80% | $4.00 | 4% |
| Quiz | 92% | $4.60 | 4.6% |
| Quiz | 100% | $5.00 | 5% |
| Quiz | 75% | $3.75 | 3.75% |
| Midterm Exam | 88 % | $8.80 | 8.8% |
| Final Exam | 89% | $22.25 | 22.25% |
| Term Paper | 74% | $11.10 | 11.10% |
| Class Part. | 100% | $15.00 | 15% |
| Homework | 100% | $15.00 | 15% |
| | | | |
| Total | | $89.5 | 89.5% |

If your teacher hasn't told you how much value each portion of the course will have, just ask. You also need to know the system you teacher uses to convert percentage grades into letters. The table below is common, but not universal.

| | |
|---|---|
| A = 98% | B = 88% |
| C = 78% | D = 68% |
| | |
| A– = 92% | B– = 82% |
| C– = 72% | D– = 62% |
| | |
| B+ = 90% | C+ = 80% |
| D+ = 70% | F = 60% |

Your teachers or your school may use different values. Ask your teachers. At the bottom of the first page of the Master Plan in your workbook, there is a chart you can use to document the method your teacher uses to determine your course grade.

WORKBOOK PRACTICE 10-9
WORKBOOK KEY WORDS
WORKBOOK PROGRESS CHECK
WORKBOOK OUTLINE

# Chapter 11 Objectives

After mastering this chapter you will be able to:

- Spot assumptions in thinking and speaking

- Identify fallacies in logic

- Use a strategy for generating ideas

# CHAPTER 11 THINK FOR YOURSELF

# Think ABOUT This

CRITICAL THINKING is a process of evaluation, one that calls for careful attention to logic and reason. It is not about being critical or putting down other people or their ideas. It's about being careful, complete, and fair. You could define **critical thinking** as *thorough* thinking.

Thinking can be a high-stakes business. People with new ideas have taken some big risks over the years. At times they have been arrested, thrown in jail, tortured, or killed. It still happens today in many parts of our world.

The way you think touches almost every aspect of your life—who you choose as friends, what you read, what you say, and how you spend time and money. There are a lot of persuasive people out there who want to sell you something. Your ability to think critically about what they say can make a big difference in your quality of life.

Publishers want you to buy their books and magazines. Television producers want you to watch their programs. Manufacturers want you to buy their products. All these people want you to agree with them. They may offer valuable ideas, products, and services, but they don't often have your best interests at heart.

Critical thinking is a tool for reaching your goals and getting what you want in life. When you know how to think critically, you can sort out what's accurate or valuable from what's half-true or a rip-off. You begin to make choices with open eyes.

WORKBOOK PRACTICE 11-1

# Start with the
# BASICS

I F YOU PRACTICE the following principles, the quality of your thinking and decision-making will improve.

Before you criticize someone's idea, make sure you understand it. See if you can state the point of view in your own words and give supporting examples.

Open up to new ideas. When you enter a discussion, be willing to change your mind. Seek out several points of view on any issue and keep looking for new answers. Ask, "What if this idea were true?" instead of "What's wrong with this idea?"

Give evidence for your ideas. Evidence includes facts and observations that support your point of view.

Some statements require no evidence. Examples are "I don't like vanilla ice cream" and "I feel happy today."

For other statements, evidence is important. Consider these assertions: "Our country needs another political party." "People have certain rights that no society can take away." "Asian students are ambitious." "You can't trust anyone over forty." "When a government no longer serves our needs, we have the right to overthrow it." These are not statements of fact, and they need to be supported by evidence.

When people refuse to think or don't know how to think, social systems can break down. Instead of solving disagreements through discussion, people resort to force. Instead of trading ideas, they exchange gunfire. When you gain skill at critical thinking, you not only sharpen your wits, you help keep the peace.

WORKBOOK
PRACTICE 11-2

# Use Questions

THINKING OFTEN INCLUDES asking and answering questions. The following ideas can help you learn to work with questions.

Choose your questions
Choose how to answer
    your questions
Write out your answers

## CHOOSE YOUR QUESTIONS

If you want to think powerfully, ask powerful questions. Vague questions lead to vague answers. Powerful questions usually have more than one answer. They also promote choice and self-responsibility. For example, compare these two paragraphs:

1. Whenever I apply for a job, I have to compete with at least fifty other people. With so many people looking for work, what chance do I have?

2. When I apply for a job, I know that employers will compare me to other applicants. What can I do to convince the interviewer that I'm a wise choice for the job?

The question at the end of paragraph #1 invites an answer: You don't have much chance at all. Answers like this can leave you feeling helpless.

The question that ends paragraph #2 invites several answers: You could learn about the company before the interview. You could ask about some of the problems this company faces. Then you could talk about how you'd help solve them. You can probably think of more. Answers like these help you take charge of your life and create options.

Here are some useful questions to ask when evaluating something:

The "journalist's question": Who? What? When? Where? How?

What's the point? What's the main idea of this article, book, or speech?

Says who? Does the person making this point have experience and training in this subject?

Is this statement logical?

What's the evidence for this statement?

Does this idea call for a change in what I think, say, or do?

What have authorities written and said about this topic?

## CHOOSE HOW TO ANSWER YOUR QUESTIONS

In addition to raising different kinds of questions, the subjects you study call for different ways of finding answers. Using paper and pencil, you can solve abstract equations without leaving your seat. To complete a chemistry assignment, however, you might have to go to the lab and use a microscope. And if you were an anthropologist like Margaret Mead or Dorothy Lee, you'd travel the world to study members of other cultures.

Some questions call only for the ability to think clearly. Others require careful observation. Many subjects require both abilities. Decide whether the answers to your key questions require clear thinking, observation, or some combination of both.

## WRITE OUT
## YOUR ANSWERS

Critical thinking and writing fit together. Writing gives you the chance to examine and revise your own thinking. When you write, the quality of your thinking is revealed. It becomes easier to spot assumptions and errors in your thinking.

It's also easier to fool yourself when speaking than when writing. You can test this by listening to a speech and then studying the written transcript. What sounds witty and intelligent from the podium might look incomplete or inaccurate in print.

To get the most benefit from writing your answers, go beyond Key Words, and examine complete sentences. Complete sentences have both a noun and a verb.

Say that you're asked to write a paper about how to listen effectively. You might brainstorm the following list of Key Words.

Attention
Patience
Learning

This list is a fine start. To refine your ideas, use these words in sentences. For example:

If you want to listen well, begin by paying close attention to the speaker.

When listening, be patient and give the speaker time to express her views.

When you are willing to learn, you will listen more closely.

Remember that asking quality questions is just as important as finding answers. Most students can answer questions. Skillful students ask questions that take their thinking down new paths.

# Dig Out Assumptions

**A**SSUMPTIONS ARE STATEMENTS that we take for granted as being true. They underlie much of what we do and say. **Assumptions** can be useful. Shared assumptions save time and make it easier for people to communicate.

We assume that the city bus driver is a skilled driver and that she knows her route well. Imagine if each passenger interviewed the driver before they took a seat: "How long have you been driving a bus? Do you know where the corner of Fifth and Longfellow is? Could I see your license?"

Holding onto outdated or false assumptions can be dangerous: "Only homosexuals and drug users get AIDS. You can't get cancer from chewing tobacco. Seat belts are dangerous because they trap people in cars."

Assumptions can also become invisible. We might accept certain ideas for so long that we even forget they are assumptions.

Here is a sample paragraph as an example:

*The 1960's was a memorable time for popular music. During this decade, rock music reached its creative heights. So far, the bands of the 1990's have failed to create music that will be remembered in thirty years.*

The paragraph is loaded with assumptions, such as:

The history of popular music can be neatly divided into ten-year periods.

Some rock music is more creative than other music.

Only the most creative music will be remembered in thirty years.

We can predict how long today's music will remain popular.

Perhaps you agree with all of these statements; perhaps you agree with only one or two of them. In any case, it's important to get assumptions out in the open. Test them. Ask for **evidence**.

Thinking for yourself includes digging out assumptions. Imagine that assumptions are everywhere, ready to confuse you. Your job is to discover which assumptions are useful and accurate. Expose faulty and misleading assumptions before they play any more tricks with your mind.

WORKBOOK
PRACTICE 11-4

WORKBOOK
JOURNAL 11-5

# Don't Fall for Fallacies in Logic

**A** FUN AND PRACTICAL part of logic is the study of fallacies. Fallacies are simply mistakes in reasoning. Once you know something about fallacies, you'll find them n many places—speeches, articles, advertisements, conversations, and more.

Some of the most common logical fallacies are described here.

## ALL-OR-NOTHING LANGUAGE

When people think in all-or-nothing terms, they imply that there are only two ways of viewing the world or only two alternatives to choose from. Some examples of **all-or-nothing thinking** include:

"Some people make it in life and some people don't. Either you're lucky or you're not."

"You're either with me or against me."

"Poor people are just lazy."

"Politicians are crooks."

## BEGGING THE QUESTION

To **beg the question** is to avoid answering it, usually by talking about the question and the issue or by stating the question in different words. Suppose you ask a state legislator whether the legal drinking age should be eighteen or twenty-one.

The legislator replies, "Thank you for asking that question. There is no one more concerned about the health and safety of our young people than I am. As your elected representative, I consider this to be an extremely important issue that deserves our most serious attention."

That's a lot of words with no answer to your question. All the legislator said was that he thinks the issue is important.

## ATTACKING THE PERSON

"Dad doesn't like my baggy clothes, but what does he know? He's too old to have a clue." Instead of talking about clothing, the speaker attacks his father's age. Again, the real question is being avoided.

## FALSE CAUSE

Consider this statement: "As people gain a bigger vocabulary, they get more cavities." The statement may be true, but not for the reason it implies. It leads us to believe that the more words we know, the more cavities we'll have. Actually, there are other factors that cause cavities.

## APPEALS TO AUTHORITY

Appeals to authority boil down to this statement: "Just about every important person agrees with me, so you should agree with me too." Here someone asks us to accept an idea just because an expert or celebrity says it's true.

You can disarm appeals to authority. For example, if you hear a TV announcer say, "Nine out of ten doctors recommend Brand X to get rid of headaches," you can ask yourself:

"Who is making this claim?"
"How was the survey conducted?"
"How many doctors were
    interviewed?"
"What were the other brands
    in the survey?"

## JUMPING TO CONCLUSIONS

Think about the following statement. "I had this teacher before and I didn't like the class. I'm sure I won't like this one, either." The speaker is assuming that every course from a particular teacher will be the same. Actually, this student might have totally different experiences in the two courses.

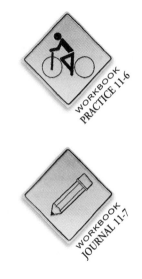

WORKBOOK
PRACTICE 11-6

WORKBOOK
JOURNAL 11-7

# Create!

CRITICAL THINKING CALLS for the ability to create ideas as well as refine them. The chapter on writing offers an example. When you write the first draft of a paper, it pays to get as many ideas written down as you can without stopping to ask, "Does this make sense?" If you ask this question too soon, you could end up with writer's block. Later, when you revise and edit your paper, you can look for mistakes in grammar, rearrange paragraphs, and rewrite unclear sentences.

## CREATIVE VS. CRITICAL

Imagine that you have two hats—one labeled "**creative thinking**" and the other labeled "**critical thinking**." The trick is knowing when to wear each hat and to avoid wearing both hats at the same time. Most people find it hard to be creative and critical. Our thinking becomes more efficient and enjoyable when we separate these two functions.

This article is about "first draft," or creative thinking. Use the techniques explained below to generate lots of new ideas. Think for quantity before you worry about quality.

## ALLOW YOURSELF TO FAIL

Creative people expect to fail. They understand that ninety-nine "crazy" ideas might come before the one that finally works. Think of failure as delayed success.

When you create a first draft, novelist Natalie Goldberg advises that you say to yourself, "I am free to write the worst junk in the world." That's another way of allowing for failure.

## CARE FOR YOUR IDEAS

Keep a record of your ideas by jotting them down as they occur to you—even when you're on the run. Keep some 3x5 cards and a pen in your pocket, purse, or backpack. Place some 3x5 cards in other key places too—your desk, your bedroom, or the bathroom. When an idea races into your mind, capture it quickly using Key Words. Later, at your leisure, expand your original notes into complete sentences.

The topic and thesis statement for your next term paper might come when you're taking a shower or fixing a snack. You can be ready.

## INCUBATE IDEAS

Ideas are like eggs. They often need time before they're ready to "hatch."

Experiment with this yourself. The next time you're stumped by a problem, tackle it in two stages.

First, focus on the problem with full attention, examine the problem from several angles, state it in several different ways, also brainstorm at least ten possible solutions.

Second, let go of the problem completely. For the moment, forget all about it. Do something else. Take a nap, listen to music, do some homework, call a friend, or go for a walk.

Some people might think you're ignoring the problem. Actually, you're incubating solutions in your subconscious mind, even while you're doing something that seems unrelated. Be prepared for a perfect solution to pop into your mind at an odd time.

## DRAW PICTURES

Switching from words to pictures helps us use different parts of our brain. Ideas that sound bulky and clumsy in words can leap to life as sketches, doodles, or drawings. Even when you can express a concept clearly in words, you might find that creating a simple chart or diagram gives you a fresh perspective.

## ASK LEADING QUESTIONS

Questions have power to focus our attention and redirect our thinking. Posing some "off the wall" questions about a subject could unleash your most creative thinking.

Especially useful are questions that start with the words *what if.* For example, Einstein asked, "What if I could ride on a beam of light? What would I see? How would I measure time?" This "thought experiment" resulted in his theory of relativity and changed physics forever.

WORKBOOK PRACTICE 11-8

WORKBOOK JOURNAL 11-9

# Play with Ideas

**N**EW IDEAS SEEM to spring out of nowhere. Actually, those ideas probably got a lot of help from thinking that's already been done. Some of the most fruitful new ideas come from putting two old ones together. Whole new subjects—like art history and biochemistry—are created this way. Creative people enjoy making new connections.

One way to create new ideas is to take old ideas and play with them. Imagine taking an idea in your hands, softening it, molding it, and turning it inside out or upside down.

Consider the paragraph that appeared earlier in the chapter: (Key Words are in **bold** type.)

*The **1960's** was a memorable time for popular music. During this decade, rock music reached its **creative heights**. So far, the **bands of the 1990's** have failed to create music that will be remembered in thirty years.*

To test the truth of this paragraph, create some new points of view by playing with the Key Words in the above sentences. Begin by stating the opposite point of view. Simply take Key Words in the paragraph and reverse them:

The **1990's** has been a memorable time for popular music. During this decade, rock music has reached **creative heights**. The **bands of the 1960's** failed to create music that is remembered in thirty years.

Think about the paragraph you just created. What evidence can you find to support it? For example, you might name specific bands from the 1990's and discuss which of their recordings might still be played and admired in thirty years.

Another way to play with the original paragraph is to reword it a little. Read the paragraph carefully, and you'll see that it's filled with bold claims. The author of these sentences is making statements about all the bands of the 1960's and comparing them to all the bands of the 1990's. That's pretty daring! It's hard to say something that's true of all bands in any period, since bands are so different.

So, consider softening the original claims:

> The 1960's was a memorable time for popular music. During this decade, **some** rock music reached its **creative heights**. **Some** of the bands of the 1990's have failed to create music that will be remembered in thirty years.

This paragraph is more cautious than the original. It is probably more accurate. It's reasonable to assume that some bands of both the 1960's and the 1990's will be remembered in thirty years.

Stating opposites and softening claims are just two ways to play with ideas and create new ones.

WORKBOOK PRACTICE 11-10

# Contemplate Art

THINKING ABOUT ART creates special challenges. When we view a painting, go to a play, listen to music, or read a novel, we don't look for fallacies in logic or dig out assumptions. Instead, we learn to experience the world through the artist's eyes and ears. The artist succeeds when we are moved by the experience.

Your teachers might ask you to write about a novel, critique a poem, or review a film. Following are questions to guide your thinking.

- Was the artist's purpose to entertain? to inform? to persuade? or to educate?

- How well did the artist achieve this purpose?

- Was the purpose worthwhile? Does this work of art help our society appreciate or understand the world in an important way?

# Fuel Your Thinking with the Three P's

FOR HIGH-OCTANE creative thinking, look to three main sources: publications, people, and personal experience. For example, if you are writing a paper about teenage parents in high school, you could seek information from the following sources.

## PUBLICATIONS

Start with the library. Look for books, articles, and pamphlets about teenage parents. Remember nonprint materials, too, such as audiotapes, videotapes, and film. You can ask a librarian for help.

Much of the information you want will come from existing materials. Begin your research here. Reading can give you a solid base of knowledge about almost any topic.

## PEOPLE

Talking with people can take you to the heart of a subject. Teenage parents in your school district could be perfect sources for your paper.

With help from teachers, counselors, and friends, create a list of the names of teenage parents. Next, contact your sources directly over the phone. Explain the reason for your call. Ask if they'd be willing to answer a few questions about their experiences as parents who are also students. Ask if they'd mind being quoted in your paper. Including quotations from sources can make your writing more meaningful.

## PERSONAL EXPERIENCE

Many researchers stop with people and publications. If you've got time, go further. Make yourself a primary source. If you are writing about figure skating, put on a pair of skates and hit the ice for an hour.

Of course, it's not always possible, or even wise, to experience a topic directly. Your paper on teenage parents is a case in point. Yet you could come closer to this subject in a number of ways. For instance, spend a day or two baby-sitting a toddler. For a limited time, try juggling homework and childcare. Then reflect on your experience and include those ideas in your paper.

WORKBOOK PRACTICE 11-11

# Make **Skillful** Decisions

A S A TEENAGER you're bombarded with opportunities to make decisions. Many of these decisions are new, and many have major consequences. There are decisions about people—whom to be friends with, what to do for fun when you're with friends, and whether to get involved in romantic relationships. There are decisions about school—which subjects to take, how to relate school to your interests, and how to make peace with grades and tests. Waiting in the wings are decisions about possible careers and what to do after high school.

Experimenting with the following suggestions can help you gain skill at decision-making.

## USE YOUR HEAD

Many people feel stuck when they begin thinking about a major decision. One option is to put thoughts on paper. Writing helps us think logically, sort out the facts, and get a handle on the costs and benefits.

As you begin, write the decision as a question: "Shall I go out with Kyle?" "Can I manage a part-time job along with all my homework?" "Would it be wise to take a math course next semester?" When you frame your decision as a question, you invite answers.

Next, brainstorm a long list of answers. Describe the short-range and long-range consequences of each answer. Look at it in terms of one week, one month, or one year from now. You could even assign point values to each answer, based on how many advantages and disadvantages it has.

## LISTEN TO YOUR HEART

Stating your question and writing about possible answers can give you a fresh understanding of the decision you face. You might even find that one answer makes more sense than all the rest.

But now you face another question: "Do I go with the answer that seems the most logical?" Sometimes the solution that seems most practical just doesn't feel right. That's an important feeling to note. Philosophers, artists, and scientists have written about the role of hunches, intuition, and just plain guesses in their work. They know the value of thinking with their hearts.

Knowing all the facts and options doesn't always lead to a clear decision. Give it some time. Often a question will answer itself when we allow it time to simmer. We can then find a solution that satisfies both the heart and the head.

## ASK, "WHO'S DECIDING HERE?"

Making decisions can be hard work. Some teens let friends or current trends do their thinking for them. Though it might seem easier in the short run, going along with the crowd puts others in charge of your life.

Making your own decisions can be easier if you think about how to announce those decisions. You can do this without attacking others. It's one thing to say, "I don't drink alcohol. I just don't like the way it makes me feel." That conveys respect for yourself. Saying "People who drink are idiots just looking for trouble" puts others on the defensive.

For more help with talking about your decisions, see the article on I-messages on pages 94-95.

## STICK WITH YOUR DECISIONS

If you decide to study algebra three days each week between 3:00 and 4:00 p.m., this also means you've decided not to watch TV or hang out with friends during that hour. You can always review your original decisions and even make new ones later. After one month you might decide to shift your algebra homework to Tuesday and Thursday nights. Until then, give your original decision a fair trial.

## INVITE OTHERS TO MAKE DECISIONS

If you listen closely when your friends talk, you might hear decisions in disguise. "I wish I could get better grades in English." "I'd feel a lot more organized if I cleared all the junk out of my room." "If I had some idea about what I wanted to do after high school, it sure would be easier to choose courses."

When you hear comments like these, invite your friends to make a decision: "Can you set a date to clean your room?" "Are you willing to talk to your English teacher about your grade?" "Can you list all the things you know you *don't* want to do after high school?"

Clear decisions lead to effective action. Encouraging your friends to recognize and make decisions helps them reach their goals.

WORKBOOK
PRACTICE 11-12

WORKBOOK
JOURNAL 11-13

WORKBOOK
KEY WORDS

WORKBOOK
OUTLINE

WORKBOOK
PROGRESS CHECK

# Chapter 12 Objectives

After mastering this chapter you will be able to:

- **BEGIN TO PLAN YOUR FUTURE**

- **CONSIDER POSSIBILITIES FOR YOUR EDUCATION AND CAREER**

- **UNDERSTAND THE VALUE OF CONTRIBUTION**

# CHAPTER LOOK AHEAD **12**

# Create Your Future

A S YOU EXPERIENCE this final chapter of *Learning Power*, return to some of the questions posed near the beginning of the book. What do you want to be doing in five years? What do you want to have? What kind of person do you want to be?

When you're willing to create a vision for the future and to begin planning your life, you can prepare for an exciting adventure. Setting goals and achieving them leads you to experience the pleasure and satisfaction of taking charge of your life.

Many people spend more time planning a vacation than they spend planning their lives. They don't even want to hear the word planning. "I don't want my life planned out," they say. "I want to be free. People who plan too much don't have any fun."

This is a common misunderstanding. Actually, planning can help you be *more* free—not less. Planning helps you make decisions that affect the future. When you know what you want to do in one month, one year, five years, or even more, you can make wiser choices today. If you leave these decisions to chance, it makes your day-to-day choices more difficult and you can end up with fewer options and less freedom.

## PLANNING IS CREATING

You may think planning is like predicting—guessing about what will happen in the future based on present trends. This is like forecasting the weather.

Planning is more like creating the future. Instead of assuming that current trends are stable, we can change those trends and even create new ones. We can choose to learn different skills, master new areas of knowledge, meet new people, and put new forces in motion.

## THINK LONG-TERM

Planning long-term means thinking months, years, and even decades into the future. By making long-term decisions now, you'll find that your short-term choices will fall in line with less effort.

## WRITE COMPREHENSIVE GOALS

Perhaps you know people who pour most of their effort and creative energy into one area. They excel at sports, chemistry, or music, yet they flounder when it comes to solving personal problems or making friends.

You can avoid such one-sided development by writing comprehensive goals. Create a vision for all aspects of your life—school, work, family, friends, hobbies, finances, health, recreation, and more.

## BE SPECIFIC

When setting goals, be very specific. For example, if you plan to meet new people, describe their attributes and interests. If you want to write a book, set dates for finishing individual chapters. When you create a goal with details, you're halfway there.

## PLANS CHANGE

The plan for your life will probably go through many drafts as you learn more about yourself and the world. Plan with the freedom of knowing that you can change any part of your plan at any time.

## PUT IT IN WRITING

Get your plan down on paper. This makes it easier to revise your plan, and it also clarifies your thinking.

## MASTER THE LEARNING PROCESS

The Mastery Learning techniques in this book will help whenever you want to learn something—at home and on the job, as well as in school.

Visionary people in industry and business stand together on one point: Knowing how to learn is about the most practical skill you can have. Chances are good that you will change careers several times in your life. Even if you stay in one field, you'll probably do several kinds of jobs within that field. Most work environments will require constant learning.

Your plans might not include education beyond high school. If you do go further, you face many choices— everything from vocational/technical schools to colleges and graduate programs. And you might change your mind several times before settling on a direction.

Mastery Learning keeps your options for the future open while doing poorly in school might rule out the chance to get a job or degree you want.

## LIST CHOICES YOU'VE ALREADY MADE

Many students have no idea of what they want to do in five years. Yet it's likely that they've already made many choices affecting their futures five years from now.

See if this is true for you. Go to the library and ask for help in finding a list of common job titles. Make a copy of the list and cross out all the jobs you definitely do not want to do. Don't be surprised if you eliminate most of the list. You have already made your choice about those careers.

## JUST CHOOSE

If you're unsure about what you want for the future, that's fine. Your planning might reveal two, three, five, or even ten possible directions for your life. If that is the case, don't worry about making the "right" choice. Just choose one. Start on something. Doing nothing or operating without a plan will likely take you away from the range of **options** that will be open in your future.

# Consider Life After Graduation

CHOOSING WHAT you'll do after high school might be easier if you think about how you want yourself to be used—how you would like to invest your time and energy. Thinking in terms of the following four categories can help you plan what you do during and after high school.

Learning and personal
    development
Job or career
Service to others
Personal life: family, friends,
    health, leisure, and entertainment

These four types of activity occur in varying degrees at every stage of your life. Some activities fit into more than one category. For example, you learn while you work. During school years more time is usually spent learning than working. When people become adults, the ratio shifts. You get to decide how much of your energy will be consumed in each area.

One option after high school is to get more schooling, either in college or in a professional training course. Or you can work fulltime, devoting less time to formal learning. There are many other ways of combining learning with working, service, and personal interests. Plan now, based on what you do well, what you enjoy, what you would like to be able to do in the future, and how much money you or your family will be able to provide.

## COLLEGE COULD BE FOR YOU

Maybe you don't see yourself as a college student or as working in the types of jobs that college graduates generally get. Remember that your choices aren't limited by what you know today or what you or members of your family have done in the past.

You can grow into the job. The longer you work in a particular field, the more you will probably be like the other people who work in that field. The people you work with on a daily basis become your teachers.

In college you will spend several years focusing on personal development instead of earning money and gaining job experience. You will learn more about yourself and the world, a benefit to both your personal and professional life.

There are financial rewards too. College graduates, on average, earn about $700,000 more during their lifetimes than people who don't graduate from college. People with college degrees often hold jobs that are more interesting and satisfying. Few people who go to college regret having done so, and often people who didn't go wish they had.

Cost can be a big barrier to going to college. Often it is easier to afford college when you are younger, before you have children to support. And even if you don't have children, leaving a full-time job to return to school can be very tough financially.

Another barrier to entering college is lack of skill to handle the work. Some students don't know how to study, others don't like to study, and some are afraid of failure. You can use the methods in *Learning Power* to gain more success in school. As you do, you may notice that your attitudes toward school and college change.

## CAREERS AND TRAINING

College is required if you want to be a nurse or a doctor, an engineer or a scientist, a lawyer, a teacher, a professor, or an architect. And college, though not absolutely required, is still an advantage in careers such as police work, sales, politics, and banking.

Training required for many career fields is available in vocational/technical programs. These career or job-oriented programs are often offered by community colleges. Others are offered at private vocational schools and academies. Some of the jobs they can prepare you for are listed on the following page.

Electronics repair
Computer operator
Computer programmer
X-ray technician
Medical technician
Emergency medical technician
Police officer
Firefighter
Drafter
Bookkeeper
Carpenter
Plumber
Electrician
Hair Stylist
Secretary
Machinist
Mechanical technician
Auto mechanic
Truck driver
Heavy equipment operator
Graphic artist
Photographer

WORKBOOK
JOURNAL 12-2

WORKBOOK
PRACTICE 12-3

# Cross the Finish Line

COLLEGE MAY NOT BE APPROPRIATE for some students and the careers they seek. But nearly everyone involved in guiding and advising teenagers recommends completing high school or passing the test for a General Education Diploma (GED).

A great deal of learning in high school takes place outside the content of courses. High school helps you learn how to learn and how to handle yourself as a young adult. You will benefit from these skills for a lifetime, whether or not you go to college.

Many students drop out of high school because they aren't learning these skills. Others quit because of drugs, crime, pregnancy, money, or family problems. If you are facing any of these issues, there are people who can help you figure out your best move. Talk privately with your teacher, your adviser, or another adult.

Dropping out of high school reduces your choices. Many careers and educational opportunities are open only to high school graduates. Another big disadvantage of dropping out is that you miss the opportunity to practice being successful. Since school is the main activity of most teens—their full-time job—finishing high school is one measure of success.

# Contribute

*LEARNING POWER* has encouraged you to look at yourself, to log your successes, and to tell the truth about your progress. You have been invited to practice new ways of reading, taking notes, writing papers, solving math problems, and much more. The idea h as been to attain the power to seize your opportunities for happiness and achievement. The focus has been on you, your effectiveness, and your success.

Focusing almost entirely on yourself—spending your time filling yourself up with knowledge and new experiences—may seem a little selfish.

Consider expanding your interests beyond yourself. People who love their work very often say that the most satisfying part of their jobs is the chance to help other people or "the opportunity to do something that makes a difference."

Ask yourself, "How can I solve problems in a way that helps other people? How can I **contribute**?"

When we hear the word *contribute*, donating money often comes to mind. Giving money is an important way to create value for others. Equally satisfying is giving our time and effort to a project we consider worthwhile.

When you begin to give, you will likely discover a deep source of joy. You might start by **volunteering** your time to organizations that support your values. You could visit nursing home residents, volunteer at a hospice, clean house or mow the lawn for a sick neighbor, or tutor a fellow student. You could join a group that's committed to saving the rain forests or ending hunger.

Perhaps one of your courses will give you a chance to do a community service project. These experiences could become the most memorable parts of your schooling.

Doing voluntary work, even for just a few hours a week, can greatly expand your sense of possibility or even lead you to a new career choice. When you contribute to others, everyone wins. You are gaining new information and skills at the same time you are helping to ease the suffering of people and the planet.

Many acts of contribution take no money and very little time. Open the door for someone in a wheelchair, haul a load of groceries up the stairs for an older person, or help find a lost child.

If you have no time or money to give, you can contribute through a third level—the kind of person you are. If you know how to listen well, speak effectively, reach agreements, and let go of resentments, many people will enjoy just being around you. Everything you say and do can become a contribution.

WORKBOOK
JOURNAL 12-4

# Make the End a Beginning

WORKBOOK JOURNAL 12-5

WORKBOOK JOURNAL 12-6

WORKBOOK KEY WORDS

WORKBOOK OUTLINE

WORKBOOK PROGRESS CHECK

L EARNING *POWER* IS MEANT to be read more than once. It can serve you long into the future. But no book has the final word about how to learn. The longer you live, the more you'll teach yourself about how to succeed in every area of your life. As you do, consider these final suggestions:

Change the ideas explained in this book to fit yourself. Invent new techniques and even plan your own book on how to learn.

If you find that a suggestion in this book doesn't work, put it on hold for now and come back to it later. A "useless" idea today might be just what you want a year from now.

The workbook can be a record of what you've learned. Review it from time to time to see how far you've come in gaining new skills. Celebrate your accomplishments.

Whatever you do in life, practice Mastery Learning. Use the cycle of planning, preparing, practicing, and getting feedback to master any new skill or subject. You can keep on learning for as long as you keep on breathing.

Live as if you were
to die tomorrow.
Learn as if you
were to live forever.

–GANDHI

# INDEX